Balanced Living

for

Busy Bahá'ís

By the same author
  Firesides (Catherine Samimi)

BALANCED LIVING

FOR

BUSY BAHÁ'ÍS

by

Catherine Brooker

Illustrations by
Gillian Nix

George Ronald
Oxford

George Ronald, *Publisher*
46 High Street, Kidlington, Oxford OX5 2DN

*A catalogue record for this book is available
from the British Library*

ISBN 0–85398–483–2

Printed in Great Britain by
The Cromwell Press Ltd, Trowbridge, Wilts

Contents

Foreword

The Bahá'í Faith is truly a global religion. Its prayers, principles and promises are for all people, regardless of race or nationality. A Bahá'í travelling to a foreign land, without knowing the native language, is comforted when he is greeted with a familiar 'Alláh-u-Abhá' upon meeting local Bahá'ís.

Bahá'í authors are traditionally very sensitive to the variety of people that constitute the extended family of the Bahá'í Faith. We strive to address our materials to the broadest audience whenever possible. This book on time and life management, however, is directed primarily towards the citizens of the western developed nations where hurry sickness and time stress are epidemic.

To any Bahá'í brethren not prone to saying 'I don't have time!', you have my utmost admiration. The people for whom this book is written already recognize themselves in the title.

Introduction

Getting the Most from This Book

If you wanted to read for purely entertainment purposes right now, you might have a romance novel or murder mystery in your hands. Instead, you are holding a non-fiction book, specifically, a self-help book. It would be a reasonable conclusion, then, to say that you desire improvements in the time management areas of your life and that you are willing to make some degree of change. Right? Let's get started.

Do you know why there are so many diet books and time management books on the market? People read them and don't do anything with the information they've read! The market is always hot for new diet or time management books. *Reading* a diet and exercise book does not make you slim and healthy. You actually have to get out of your chair and do the exercises described in the book! The same is true with time management books. If you really want to see improvements in your life, then you must challenge yourself to implement the parts of the book that resonate with you. Writing things down is an essential part of good time and life management.

To truly benefit from this book, you will need a notebook and pen at your side. While reading, you will have numerous idea flashes that are uniquely applicable to your life. Use the notebook for your inspirational 'notes to self'. A piece of paper will not do. You really will write more than that. If you read something you like and say, 'Yeah, that sounds good!' and carry on reading, you will forget the point that inspired you for a moment. Your notebook is for the highlights that you want to remember and weave into your life. There will also be a few exercises to do and you will need your notebook for those too. For most note-taking situations I recommend a ring binder with pages that can be removed. This allows you to move pages about, throw some away or file them.

As you read, write down the techniques you want to see working in your life. Then commit to doing them. Review your list every day. Be patient with yourself, as permanent change happens when new ideas are integrated gradually. You might organize your clothes closet to glowing perfection today but the habits that got it disorganized are still inside you. The closet will be chaos again within a week unless you are consciously practising your new habits.

One Day at a Time

Remember, change doesn't have to be elaborate and it need not come all at once. Take it one day at a time. 'Just for today I will hang up my clothes and not put them on the chair or the floor.' 'Just for today I will write phone numbers and messages in my notebook and not on scraps of paper.' If you start a filing system at home, vow to put every piece of paper you handle in its place, just for today. Tomorrow you can go back to the piling system if you must but today you will file.

Soon you will find yourself preferring to do things

the new ways. They are becoming your new habits! *Gradual* change has the best hope of permanency, whether it be with weight loss or time management. Radical fast changes seldom last. Gradual ones do.

I encourage you to take a one-month trial with this book. Make a commitment to yourself to implement the new strategies you learn for a one-month period. If at the end of one month you don't like sleeping better, not hurrying and feeling peaceful inside, you can always return to being disorganized and hurried if you miss it! But first give the new strategies for living an honest effort for one month. You could be stunned by the results.

Start practising the new standards you want to live by immediately, without waiting until you've finished reading the whole book. That's a form of procrastination too. 'I'll get organized after I've read the book.' Start now. Becoming the master of your time may well be the single most important gift you give yourself.

Balanced Living for Bahá'ís

Few time management books ever mention God and they certainly don't mention any particular religion. Why is that? Mainly to sell more books. The more mainstream a book is, the more copies will sell, which is an understandable business decision. This book is different. Worshipping God and obeying Him are central to Bahá'í life. Being a Bahá'í and serving Bahá'u'lláh *do* have daily implications on a Bahá'í's time. This is a time and life management book specifically and unabashedly written for Bahá'ís.

1

Time Stress

Busy-ness

How busy is your life?

Are you employed outside the home? Do you work inside the home? Do you work both *in* and *out* of the home? Do you serve on a Bahá'í Assembly or committee? Do you hold firesides, facilitate a study circle and go travel teaching? Do you attend Nineteen Day Feasts, Holy Days and other Bahá'í events? Do you live with other people (spouse/children/roommate)? Do you do volunteer work for non-Bahá'í organizations? Do you spend time commuting? Do you exercise? Do you have a social life?

In the western world we live in a culture where people feel increasingly over-extended. We are a busy society. Add to all your individual responsibilities a personal commitment to something, such as crusading for the environment or serving the Bahá'í Faith, and it is highly probable that your life has a busy momentum about it. If you picked up this book because the title intrigued you, there likely is a degree of busy-ness about your life that does not feel right to you.

'I don't have time!' Have you ever heard yourself say that? Probably several times a week. 'If only I had another hour, even 20 minutes, I could get more done!' But more time is not the answer. If by some miracle your days permanently changed to 25 hours, your life would not be any different. You would still be surrounded by your current flurry of activity, with no noticeable appreciation of the extra entire hour added to each day.

'Time management' is a misnomer. We don't actually manage time. The clock goes on ticking, oblivious to our needs and how we feel about time. Practically speaking, in time management we are actually learning to better manage *ourselves*.

> The day is of infinite length
> for him who knows how to appreciate and use it.
> *Goethe*

Role Models

I used to be far too busy, mostly because I voluntarily took on too much. When I realized my life needed a time management overhaul, I decided to look at my role models and observe how they managed their time. I looked at the people I respect and asked myself, 'Who do I admire for their time management skills?' I was shocked by the answer – no one. Not one time management role model! There are people I greatly admire for different segments of their lives. One person is very athletic and sets a good example for healthy living. Another is a dedicated servant of the Faith who ceaselessly gives to others. I have many role models for different things. Yet not one of these people is living what I would call an integrated and well-balanced life.

The athlete – yes, he has a great body – can't seem to stay in a steady relationship or a steady job. The woman who serves the Faith so tirelessly is overweight and would rather go to more Bahá'í meetings than give one hour to exercise. Many of my 'role models' who are high achievers in specific areas of their lives (professionally or in Bahá'í service) also have spouses and children who feel neglected. I asked myself: Is it so impossible to lead a balanced life?

I silently observed the crowd during the social time of one particular Nineteen Day Feast. The adults reminded me of a hive of busy bees, getting their business done. It was Bahá'í business but nonetheless it was business. 'Abdu'l-Bahá says, 'It is my hope that this feast will be given on one day out of every nineteen, for it bringeth you closer together; it is the very well-spring of unity and loving-kindness.'[1] Where do the writings say 'and hold a mini committee meeting in the corner' or 'frantically recruit people for your projects'? Many of the adults at this Feast looked seriously stressed!

The children, on the other hand, were holding a different kind of social time. They were sitting on the floor eating cake. They were laughing and enjoying each others' company. I imagined 'Abdu'l-Bahá attending this Feast. I could not picture Him dashing around the room with His clipboard, talking fast and persuading people to sign up for something. I imagined He would have sat with the cake-eaters.

'Abdu'l-Bahá is one of my role models. I try to imagine Him living in our modern world amidst all its busy-ness. Would He succumb to its hectic pace? I believe not. The Master knew how to live *in* the world but not be *of* the world.

Not having a living role model for a well-managed life was a serious warning signal for me – a serious societal concern as well. But before I could worry about the state of the nation I had to first fix the problem closer to home. If I could not find a suitable living role model for time management, then I would have to become that person myself. In a place where busy sickness, stress and fatigue have taken over our culture, I would try to create a peaceful, unhurried, yet productive life for myself.

People in other cultures do it. Remote tribes spend an average of 17 hours a week gathering food. Much of the remaining time is used for leisure. Here we are in the industrialized world with all the 'benefits' of technology, working 40 to 60 hours a week. We are chronically sleep-deprived and we continually feel behind with our tasks. We have become slaves of materialism. I'm not suggesting we give up all our possessions and move into the wilderness. I do believe it is possible to live in the modern world without becoming encumbered by all its trappings.

Superwoman

Let's look closely at one person who has a well-established reputation for being too busy. Her name is Superwoman. Perhaps you've met her. Perhaps you're trying to be her.

Superwoman is often a mother who also has a full-time or part-time job outside the home. She is usually the primary parent, cook, laundry maid, chauffeur and all-round domestic manager. She exercises at the gym regularly and can host a dinner party on a moment's notice. She does all this with a smile on her face and not a hair out of place.

Have you ever heard of Super*man*? He's a comic-book hero with a big 'S' on his chest. He wears blue tights and a cape. He flies through the air faster than a speeding bullet and leaps tall buildings in a single bound. Superman, however, doesn't have to stop saving the world from evil at 3:30 p.m. so he can pick up the kids after school.

There is no Superman. My point is that there is no Superwoman either. If you still think she exists and you're trying to be just like her, you are living in your own deluded cartoon. It is humanly impossible to do all the things attributed to Superwoman's prowess. Being super-successful in every corner of your life simultaneously is simply not possible. You can keep it up for a while, or give the impression that you are coping, but in very short order something will crash.

If you are a parent (especially a single parent) accept that your kids will be an all-consuming priority for the next several years. Keeping them safe, warm and fed is your labour of love. But don't also try to keep up with all your friends who don't have children at home. You simply can't go to as many meetings, attend as many aerobics classes or maybe even advance in the workplace at the same speed as they do. If the latest advertisements suggest to you that Superwomen exist, they are marketing an illusion. It's part of a conspiracy to make you feel inadequate and consume more of their products.

But do not be disappointed. The good news is that you *can* have it all. Or at least you can have most of the life you desire. Just not all at the same time. Some of our achievements have to be sequential, not simultaneous.

If you know someone who has succumbed to the Superwoman myth, let her know the game is over and she doesn't have to play anymore. She will be so relieved.

The Rat Race

There are numerous books and seminars designed to help people become better managers of their time and masters of their destiny. One such seminar teaches:

It's not enough to be on the right track,
you have to be going in the right direction.
It's not enough to be going in the right direction,
you have to stay ahead of the train that's behind you.

It's an amusing slogan. It's also rubbish. Who wants to be frantically chased through life? If you have to run as fast as you can to save yourself from being run over *by your own life*, something is definitely wrong. I say it's better to step completely off the fast track and walk the garden path instead. It's far more beautiful. There are no trains, either. There is another expression: 'In the rat race, the rats win.' Then the train hits them anyway.

Most time management books are directed at business managers, helping them do more things efficiently, so they can just do more and more things. I believe that time management skills are good for *everyone*, for we are all managers of our personal lives. Amazingly, with a proper time and life management overhaul, you may actually end up doing *less*. Satisfaction with one's life depends on doing what's important, not on doing everything.

2

To Be or Not To Be,
That is the Answer

*If one advances confidently in the direction of his dreams
and endeavours to live the life which he has imagined,
he will meet with success unexpected in common hours.*
Henry David Thoreau

It is common for people to wrestle with the ominous
question 'What is my purpose in life?' We have an
innate drive to do something of importance or to 'be
somebody', even if we do not yet know what we want
to do or be. For people who have religious convictions,
such as Bahá'ís do, religion serves as a reliable compass
when determining the directions to take in one's life.

The short obligatory prayer assures the Bahá'í that
'Thou hast created me to know Thee and to worship
Thee'.¹ His life plan stems from that statement. The
prayer clarifies for the Bahá'í that his primary purpose
is his own spiritual development rather than, say,
making money and climbing the social ladder.

Being a Bahá'í has distinct implications for how one
spends one's time. The Bahá'í incorporates prayer and
meditation into his daily life. Teaching the Faith is a priority. He fasts. He observes Bahá'í Holy Days and looks

forward to the Nineteen Day Feast. He arises when the institutions of the Faith call him to service and he offers his own initiatives. Throughout this book the unique roles and responsibilities of Bahá'í life are woven into practical strategies for improving one's personal time and life management.

To Be or Not To Be

> This time, like all times, is a very good one,
> if we but know what to do with it.
> *Ralph Waldo Emerson*

Before you can better organize what you do with your time, you first need to understand *why* you do the things you do. Time management is so much more than creating a 'To Do' list each morning. Why those items appear on your 'To Do' list is much more important than what those tasks actually are.

Do you write daily or weekly 'To Do' lists? If so, you're on the right track! They keep our minds and activities focused. It is so easy to have our attention taken away from what matters most in our lives. Some people scoff at lists, saying lists are for sissies. For those people, I have the following story:

Yale University conducted a study with shocking results. In 1953 students in a graduating class were asked if they had personal goals and if they had written plans of how they would achieve them. Remarkably, only three per cent answered 'yes'. Twenty years later, in 1973, the same former students were asked how much money they were worth now, compared to how much they were worth in 1953. The study found that the three per cent who had clear goals and plans were worth more (financially speaking) than the other 97 per cent combined!

Financial success was apparently an important measuring stick to the people conducting this study. Even though money may not be the most important determinant for you, there is still a lesson to be learned from this study. Simply put, *without clear and written goals, your life probably won't go where you want it to.* And what a shame that would be, to look back on your life and regret how poorly you managed it. Fortunately, those regrets are all preventable, if you sit up and plan the rest of your life, *now.*

If you dismiss the idea of writing a 'To Do' list each day, think again. No ship sets sail without a sail plan and nautical charts. You might think that you can get by one day at a time without written plans but a series of days spent at random totals up to a lifetime spent without direction. Suddenly you wake up in the latter half of your life wondering why you haven't done many of the wonderful things you told yourself you would have accomplished by now.

Who Do You Want To Be?

> I always wanted to be somebody,
> but I should have been more specific.
> *Lily Tomlin*

Before you can write effective daily 'To Do' lists, you first need to have a clearly written 'To Be' list. If you first know who you want 'to be', then what you need 'to do' in order to get there becomes clear.

So who do you want to be? Sorry, Julia Roberts and Mel Gibson are taken! But do you know what kind of *you* you want to be? If you fantasize about being your optimal self, what does your life look like?

No one writes on a 'To Be' list 'I want to be someone who does laundry once a week'. It's not a burning personal aspiration that gives life richer meaning. Yet we all have laundry to do several times a month. Personal routine chores that keep our lives afloat, like paying bills and house maintenance, are not profound but we can't ignore them. Yet if a person neglects big picture planning in life and only makes lists on a daily basis, the days are easily filled with many small housekeeping tasks. You can be busy all day long but your bigger personal goals are no further ahead. That is why long-term planning and re-evaluation are essential. It is all too easy to be kept busy with little spontaneous tasks while the larger life goals stay continually postponed.

In a moment we will do an exercise where you write down who you want to be. I assure you there are no wrong answers. Let your honest admissions all come forth. Do you want to be a doctor? A mother? An amateur hockey player? A home front pioneer? Who do you *really* want to be? Deep inside your heart you know who you'd like to be. Let your list represent who you want to be now and in the future.

Besides listing the roles you want to play in life, also list personal qualities such as 'I want to be patient/generous/a good listener/a loyal servant of Bahá'u'lláh . . .' for example. You can also list personal traits you'd like to develop, such as 'I want to have good posture' or 'I want to be a non-smoker'. I once had 'Improve the tone of my voice' on my list. For several months I paid attention to talking slower and deeper, which gave my voice a much warmer tone. (Incidentally, the film actress Lauren Bacall, who is well-known for her deep and rich voice, was once rejected for a movie role because her voice sounded too high-pitched and squeaky. She determined to improve her voice quality. Later she auditioned, unrecognized, before the same person for a different role and won the part!)

Do not shy away from having financial goals, thinking it is not spiritual to be rich. 'I want to be wealthy' is an acceptable goal. Earning money is not a sin. What you do with your acquired wealth is what counts. You can help a lot of people when you have the financial means and desire to do so.

In the introduction you were advised to prepare yourself with a notebook. You are about to write your 'To Be' list in that notebook. This is something you will likely keep for years to come and some people prefer to write this list in a good quality book. If you carry your 'To Be' list in your handheld computer, just like you carry your daily 'To Do' lists, this is great for referring to your 'to be's at any time you wish. But keeping a master copy of your 'to be's in a notebook in your own handwriting is better for a long-term record.

Now prepare to do the exercise. Sit yourself in a private and comfortable place. Open your notebook to a new page and write at the top 'I Want To Be . . .' Some people choose to write 'I am . . .' to activate these qualities in the present tense, which is fine. Some folks don't like 'I am' in cases such as 'I am a marathon runner' because walking to the end of the block currently leaves them breathless. Their marathon is likely two years away. Considering myself to be a perpetual work in progress, I use the phrase 'I aspire To Be . . .' Select the wording which suits you best.

Bullet point form is a list-making style used by many people and it works well for this exercise. Some people prefer to list their qualities in sentence form, such as 'I aspire to be a forgiving person who overlooks the short-comings of others', 'I am a tidy person who cleans up after herself right away'. When you re-read your list, and that is the point in writing it, sentences help you to visualize being the person you are striving to be.

Take 20 or 30 minutes now to write your personal 'To Be' list. If you are tempted to continue reading this book, telling yourself 'I'll do the exercise later', I assure you, you won't do it. And doing a sort-of list in your head is ineffective. You need to see your words in ink, staring back at you, for them to impact you now and in the future. You have chosen to read this book because you want some improvements in your life. Do you want to be on the sidelines reading about other people's transformations or would you actually like to be living your optimal life? So go ahead and do the exercise – NOW. The rest of the book will have more meaning for you if you do. I'll meet you back here afterwards.

If at any time you wonder whether the items on your 'To Be' list are in accordance with what Bahá'u'lláh would want for you, imagine 'Abdu'l-Bahá standing beside you, looking over your shoulder and reviewing your list with you. He'll help you write it.

No capacity is limited when led by the Spirit of God!
'Abdu'l-Bahá

Later . . .

Good for you! Isn't it exciting, seeing the person you aspire to be so clearly in written form? Keep your notebook near by. You will be making little amendments to your list as you read on.

In the movie *Fight Club*, there is a scene in which Brad Pitt's character storms into a convenience store at night and takes the shopkeeper into the back alley at gunpoint. One would think the shopkeeper was being robbed but Pitt has other plans.

He throws the shopkeeper to his knees and holds a gun to the back of his head. Pitt takes the shopkeeper's wallet and rummages through it. Upon finding an expired college ID card, Pitt demands to know what the shopkeeper had studied. The shopkeeper began an education in veterinarian medicine but quit due to the extensive studies involved.

Pitt then gives him a choice: the shopkeeper can either resume his post-secondary education or die here and now behind a convenience store. Pitt keeps the shopkeeper's driver's licence, promising to check if he has enrolled in a school or college within six weeks. If not, he will be dead. The shopkeeper is then ordered to run on home.

While I hope you never run into Brad Pitt in a darkened alley (although many women would probably like to take their chances!), imagine for a moment being that shopkeeper. A stranger with a gun is giving you the ultimatum: 'Do what you really want to do with your life . . . or I will kill you.' Would that change anything about the way you are living your life now? Sit and think about it for a moment.

The same number of days will pass by in your life-time whether or not you do the things you love. So do what you love.

Later in the movie, Brad Pitt goes home and pins Raymond's driver's licence on the back of his bedroom door for follow-up. Very briefly we see on the back of the door several other licences. This renegade char-acter makes a hobby out of scaring people into being who they really wanted to be! This is the end of that brief storyline and the film moves on to its title subject, of establishing a fight club.

Not being attracted to boxing matches myself, I was more interested in the plot that *could* have been, namely following the lives of the people represented on the back of the bedroom door. Who were these other people? What changes did they make in their lives? Did Raymond go to veterinarian school? One can only wonder.

When asked what he would do if he only had six months left to live, author Isaac Asimov replied, 'Type faster!' He was a man who was living his purpose. He found his calling as a writer and lived his life congruent with his purpose. If you had six months to live, what would you do? More of what you are already doing or would there be big changes? If 'big changes' is your answer, you just found something interesting to medi-tate on.

In 1996 I was on a much-needed vacation basking in the sun on a boat in the Caribbean. Away from my stresses and responsibilities, I was able to ask myself this all-important question: if I were at the end of my very long life, would I have any regrets about having not accomplished certain goals? The answer hit me like a giant wave coming over the deck: I want to be a writer! I want to be able to say 'I AM a writer!' I don't wanna-be a wanna-be writer!

When I returned home from that trip, I immediately started rewriting material from a workshop I had developed. I turned it into a full-length manuscript. Three years later it was published as a book called *Firesides*.

Now, return to your 'To Be' list and imagine that you are very old and reflecting back upon your entire life. Is there anything more that you need to accomplish for you to be satisfied with your life?

Aspirations shared by some people include:

I want to be a veterinarian.
I want to be an overseas pioneer.
I want to be financially independent during retirement.
I want to write children's books.
I want to be a deepened Bahá'í.
I want to be a loving spouse.
I want to be a caring steward of our planet.

Did you write down on your 'To Be' list 'My long-term goal is to become obese and inactive'? I didn't think so. Yet this is the result many people end up with. How is this possible, if obesity wasn't a written goal of theirs? It happens because *health* was not a clear and written goal. Do your best to honour the temple of your body which God has entrusted to you. Put a healthy aspiration on your 'To Be' list if it is not already there.

Next, divide the items on your list into the following categories:

- spiritual
- physical
- social
- mental
- recreational
- material

Be sure you do not end up with too many aspirations in one category, while excluding other important areas of your life. Your intention is to have your aspirations balanced in a healthy way.

One-Time Goals

Now look at your 'To Be' list again and add any lifetime accomplishments that might be missing. Include any one-time events, such as 'I want to go on pilgrimage' or 'I want to visit the Bahá'í temple in India' or 'I want to sing a solo at a Nineteen Day Feast'.

Not every goal has to be elaborate or long term. Reading a special book or taking a weekend course in something does deserve to be on your list if it resonates with who you want to be.

Do not judge the quality of your choices. If some feel self-indulgent, remember you are allowed some self-care along the way. All your goals do not have to be on the scale of saving the world. If on your near deathbed you would like to be able to say 'I learned to tango', then tango you should!

Legacy

> My greatest joy in planting is not to pluck my own fruits but to provide them for others.
> *Copernicus*

While contemplating who you aspire to be, consider what will be the legacy of your life. For what will you be remembered? Will you make any contributions to the world that will outlast you?

You don't have to leave millions of dollars in your will or find a cure for cancer in order to say that you are leaving a legacy. For example, many Bahá'ís believe that their children are their legacy. To educate and raise their offspring to become upstanding world citizens is an incredible achievement. Service to humanity by the parents is continued and hopefully surpassed by their children. Teaching the Faith can be your legacy. When you pass on, can it be said that the Bahá'í community in your country is larger and stronger partly because of your teaching efforts?

Part of my legacy is writing. Author and activist Gloria Steinem wrote, 'Writing is much more efficient. You can travel six months and not reach as many people as you can if you write one thing.' Reading this quotation was a pivotal moment for me. After *Firesides* was published, I was kept busy with public speaking engagements and regretted not having more time for writing. Reading Steinem's words was the catalyst for me to prioritize writing again. More people can read my books than I will ever meet in person and, God willing, some books will outlast me. The legacy I desire is that other people feel inspired by some things I write. The contributions these people make in the world will be far greater than my own individual efforts could ever be.

> The great use of a life
> is to spend it for something that outlasts it.
> *William James*

What will your legacy be? Which of your contributions would you like to see outlive you? Be conscious and intentional about the legacy you want to offer. Now write your desired legacy in your notebook. 'I want my legacy to be . . .'

Profession vs. Purpose

> If they can make penicillin out of mouldy bread,
> they can sure make something out of you.
> *Muhammad Ali*

When people ask themselves 'What is my purpose in life?' they often expect the answer to be in the form of a career. 'My purpose in life is to be an artist/lawyer/librarian.' How can a person possibly narrow one's reason for being into an *occupation*? A job is but one way to express oneself. Defining the purpose of life by having the perfect job, perfect relationship or lots of money is flawed because it is a human definition.

Remember, the short obligatory prayer instils in us 'Thou hast created me to know Thee and to worship Thee'. That is our purpose in life, concisely expressed. Everything else in our lives is but an extension of our purpose to know God and to worship Him. The prayer doesn't say 'Thou hast created me to become a pharmacist and be wealthy'.

Doing our best in a career is one of the ways by which we serve God. Bahá'u'lláh commands us:

> O people of Bahá! It is incumbent upon each one of you to engage in some occupation – such as a craft, a trade or the like. We have exalted your engagement in such work to the rank of worship of the one true God.[3]

Choosing one career and sticking with it throughout one's lifetime is a minority career pattern today. Most people change several times throughout their lifetime. What is a person to do if he thinks he wants to change professions mid-life?

Even though some people fantasize about a career change, following through on such a big move at the mid-point of one's life can be frightening. There are risks in starting over. You risk being wrong about the grass being greener on the other side. But you also risk being very happy and fulfilled with the change. If you are not at rest in your current job, ask yourself the following question: 'If my dream job paid the same as my current one, is there something else I would rather be doing?'

I asked this question to two teachers at the same time.

Both were quite satisfied with their teaching jobs. But each talked more passionately about things other than teaching. One had daydreams of owning his own business and the other was a very talented musician. When asked what careers they would choose if money were not a factor, one blurted out, 'I'd open a health food store!' Simultaneously the other said, 'I'd make music!' Both men froze and stared at each other. Then they laughed and embraced each other. They knew it was time to follow their passions. The two friends made a pact to do something in these directions. Not long after, the first teacher did open a health food store. The other kept teaching and released a CD of his own music.

Some people are in professions which require a considerable investment of time and money on education. These people have also worked hard to earn status in the workplace. To leave a profession at this stage feels to some like a waste of many years and a lot of money. Making a change is never a waste. It is an act of wisdom and courage.

If you are truly unhappy in your profession, ask yourself how old you were when you made your career choice. Were you 18 and starting college? If so, it is now important for you to ask: 'Would I today ask an 18-year-old to decide for me what my next career should be?' Certainly not! What does an 18-year-old know? Not enough for you to base the rest of your life on his opinion! So if you now have a different calling than you did when you were 18, you are in the majority. Many people made initial career choices based on whim, lack of clarity or what someone else wanted for them.

Some people did make very good choices when they were 18. Even if a good career choice was made, a change might still be appropriate later on. A once appealing profession has run its course and it's now time to try something else. Do you have any career adjustments to make on your 'To Be' list?

On the other hand, staying in a career that does not excite you is not necessarily bad if you have good reasons for staying in it. Your profession does not have to be your primary passion. In fact, you do not have to be in love with your job at all, as long as you do not go so far as to resent it.

I know an accountant who freely admits his work does not excite him.

'I learned a long time ago that this kind of work would never hold any lustre for me,' he says. 'I thought about changing professions but I really didn't like the thought of starting over. I am fond of the cash flow my practice provides me and I'm honest about that. That cash flow is what enables me to do all the other things I want to do. I love to travel and I do it often. My wife and I have devoted many of our trips to travel teaching. Our eldest daughter is an overseas pioneer and our other daughter finishes university next year and plans to do the same. I told them both I would help support them financially if they went overseas to serve the Cause. None of this would be possible if I didn't have a lucrative accounting practice. So although accounting itself doesn't excite me, I say "thank you" to God every day I walk into my office because I have a lot to be grateful for.'

Take one final look at your 'To Be' list. Are there any additions or subtractions to make? Once it looks complete, you are ready to proceed with determining what you need 'to do' with your time.

A once appealing profession has run its
course and its now time to try
something else.

3

Much To Do About Everything

Things which matter most
must never be at the mercy
of things which matter least.
Goethe

'To Do' Lists

This chapter will help you to look at each of your 'to be' items and discover the 'to do's that will bring them to fruition. Let's use the example of health.

Suppose you wrote 'I want to be lean, agile and healthy'. But at the moment you are carrying around 100 pounds of extra 'you'. Lean needs some work. And as for agility, well, your girth makes just tying your shoes rather difficult these days.

Achieving your health goals needs to be broken down into measurable portions. Saying 'I want to lose weight' is too vague. 'I want to lose 100 pounds this year' is clear and measurable. Divide your weight loss into realistic monthly goals and weekly fitness activities. This gives you a direction to aim for as well as the satisfaction gained by reaching small milestones along the way.

Long-Term Goals

Some goals are very long term. Suppose you want to take flying lessons. You've also told yourself you want to pay off your mortgage before permitting yourself that new and exciting, yet expensive, flying hobby. If there are nine years left on your mortgage, that means your flying lessons will not begin until nine years from now. Keep 'flying lessons' on your 'To Be' list! Since that goal is so far away you might wonder why you should bother to have it in writing. It's because *goals not written down risk never being achieved*.

Nine years from now, once the mortgage is paid, another opportunity might appear before you, such as the temptation to renovate your house. If you routinely revisit your list of goals, though, you will find yourself saying, 'Hey, wait a minute! I promised myself I could have flying lessons this year.' You will then weigh the advantages between having the house renovated and starting flying lessons. Perhaps the attraction to flying has faded away. Or perhaps it is as strong as ever and the new attraction, household improvements, should take a number and wait in line.

Some goals will take several years to accomplish. Perhaps you want to finish your degree part-time. Map out how many courses you can reasonably finish each year. What will your goals be for this year? For the next six months? This week's goal could be to call the college and request the calendar of programmes.

Eliminating Goals

When goals are broken down into their necessary subsets,

Discover the 'to do's that will bring
your 'to be's into fruition

some goals actually come *off* people's lists. Suppose 'I want to play piano' is on someone's 'To Be' list. But once it is broken down into its obligatory smaller portions, playing piano starts to look less appealing. Weekly lessons? Practising every day? Not sounding good enough to play at Feast for a few years? Suddenly the person realizes he has a fantasy of sitting at the piano and playing something beautiful but in reality he isn't willing to devote the time required to learn to play piano. Recognizing this, he gets to wipe 'I want to play piano' off his list of goals. This decision frees him from the sense of procrastination he had about starting to learn the instrument. Removing expired goals from one's 'To Be' list is very liberating!

One-Time Goals

Some goals are what we call 'one-time goals'. 'I want to go on pilgrimage' is something you might do once in your life. It is not an ongoing, state-of-being type of goal. But keep it on your 'To Be' list! Your pilgrimage will not accidentally happen to you while you are busy attending to the rest of your life. You have to plan for it. You will need to ask permission well in advance. Be specific. 'I will go on pilgrimage when my daughter starts school' is clearer than 'I want to go on pilgrimage some day'.

Changing Plans

By now you might have said to yourself, 'Can I really make so many long-term plans here and now? What if my interests change down the road?' Your interests *will* change. You will revise your goals periodically. The purpose of writing them down is not to structure your life in an inflexible fashion. The purpose of planning is to ensure that the things which are most dear to you are not continually postponed by less important but seemingly urgent daily demands on your time.

If you keep your long-term 'To Be' lists in their own separate notebook and you save this journal for many years, you will look back and see the progression of your life planning. Ideas that were once important to you are no longer on your list. But new ones are. The best reward, however, is seeing items that began as dreams, which then became plans and eventually were goals accomplished! Looking back on your 'To Be' lists from ten years ago is like reading a concise and revealing diary of your life. It reminds you of who you were and what was important to you then. That is why I recommend that your 'To Be' notebook be of good quality – because you want it to last.

So Many Choices

Once all of your 'to be's are broken down into weekly portions, check if the busy-ness of your week is realistic. If your 'to be's are too great in number and it looks like you will have to quit your full-time job just to get it all in, it's time to make some choices. Some of your 'to be's will just have to go.

I often have the problem of being attracted to many things simultaneously. Life is one big buffet of exciting opportunities. Sometimes we have to make difficult choices. If you find yourself caught in this quandary, one solution is to entitle yourself to your 'to be's *sequentially.*

For example, if you want to sing in the Bahá'í choir *and* take ballroom dancing lessons but both are on Wednesday evenings, do one of them this year and promise yourself you can do the other one next year.

Choices in Bahá'í Service

Recognizing that one cannot do everything at the same time must also apply to one's Bahá'í service. Some opportunities for Bahá'í service come to us because we are elected or appointed to serve in certain capacities. We also have our own individual initiatives we love to act upon. Other people have initiatives we want to support. There are Feasts, Holy Days, study circles, devotional meetings, teaching projects and social events that we want to be part of. All of these activities require *time*. A prudent Bahá'í must recognize how much output is realistically possible. The quality of one's service is as vital as the quantity.

As much as we may want to serve, serve, serve, the reality is that there are times when an individual CANNOT participate in all the Bahá'í projects he is attracted to simultaneously. Bahá'í service is not a race to see how fast you can burn out your own candle. That would lead to a short and imbalanced life. If you include planning and self-care in your repertoire, you will live longer and healthier, thereby maximizing the number of hours and years you can devote to the Cause. While you might feel like a 'kid in a candy store' at times with opportunities to serve the Faith, part of spiritual development includes mature decision-making.

Whenever you are torn between different opportunities for Bahá'í service, remember you can always turn

to the guidance of the institutions of the Faith. The
Universal House of Justice gives us plans from which
our national and local goals are derived. These goals
can assist us in prioritizing our personal plans.

The Importance of Planning

> If we were to do all we are capable of doing,
> we would literally astonish ourselves.
> *Thomas Edison*

Mapping out your month and week are 'to do' items in
themselves. It is necessary to block out some time on
your calendar exclusively for life planning and evaluation. Managers of businesses and governments hold
planning meetings. They strategize to attain their goals
and regularly assess whether or not they are on
schedule. People consult and business plans are
revised. Your personal life is no less important and it
too requires planning and reassessment! To assume
that everything will turn out fine in your life without
regular review leaves too much to chance and lots of
room for mishaps. If you ran a business that way you'd
be fired.

Once a month look at your 'To Be' list to ensure the items that can be acted upon do get some time on your calendar. Let's say you want 'to be a dedicated follower of the Bahá'í Faith'. This year you set a personal goal: 'To start a deepening programme in our community.' This goal could be postponed indefinitely, since there is no date attached to it that would force you to get started.

In this month's planning you could determine to:
- identify potential deepening topics
- research existing prepared materials
- send a written proposal to the Assembly

In your weekly planning you would block off time for doing each of these tasks. This leads us to the subject of project planning.

Project Planning

When you have a long-term project, such as developing a deepening programme, it does not sit as a 'to do' item for only one day. Such projects require a master 'To Do' list of their own, preferably kept in a separate file for that project.

For any ongoing project, start a file, paper or electronic, right away. Even while something is in its earliest planning stages, create a file for it. Suppose in your day-timer you have written 'Sunday 2:00–4:00: prepare deepening.' On Sunday you open up your 'Deepenings' file and inside is the 'To Do' list you prepared for that project.

Within each individual project take the time to plan. A new project can be exciting and it is tempting to start right away with a fun part. It is better to take some time at the beginning to get an overview of where you are going. Planning will save you *something* – be it time, money or disappointment.

A weekly or monthly review of projects is all that is required. To monitor the whole project at each session is a waste of time. Schedule your review and your work sessions to be at different times. Thirty minutes on Saturday will be for overall strategy planning, for example, while two hours on Sunday will be focused on getting particular tasks done. This ensures that the time you allot for actually doing the work of the project will be focused and more productive.

During your weekly personal planning time you can begin the 'To Do' lists for certain days. For example, if you know you need to contact Bob and he is out of town until Thursday, write 'phone Bob' on next Thursday's 'To Do' list now. If you have decided to exercise three times a week, choose those dates during your weekly planning time and mark them on your 'To Do' list or calendar. If left until each morning's planning time, exercise could easily be postponed until tomorrow, then another tomorrow – and you know where that goes!

Planning Firesides

The writings make our obligation to hold monthly firesides in our homes unquestionably clear:

> The friends must realize their individual responsibility. Each must hold a Fireside in his or her home, once in 19 days, where new people are invited, and where some

phase of the Faith is mentioned and discussed. If this is done with the intent of showing Bahá'í hospitality and love, then there will be results. People will become interested in 'what' you are interested in, and then be interested in studying. Individual firesides will bring the knowledge of the Faith to more people, under favourable circumstances, and thus constantly enrich its circle of friends, and finally its members. There is no substitute for the teaching work of the individual.[1]

Firesides are a good example of a recurring monthly event. I strongly recommend you open a file (paper or electronic) called 'Firesides'. In it you keep a list of current guests and those you plan to invite in the near or distant future. You keep notes to yourself, such as resource material and topics individual guests are interested in. You also keep track of the regularity of your firesides, ensuring that at least once in 19 days you have a friend in your home for the purpose of discussing the Bahá'í Faith.

Martin and Laura share their story:

> We circle the dates on our kitchen calendar that we reserve for firesides, making sure there is at least one per Bahá'í month. This is a priority for us. We both have such hectic professional lives plus two children, it gets so awkward, if not impossible, to plan an engagement together. With our fireside strategy, if one of us has a teaching opportunity during which we would like to invite the person to a fireside, we don't have to check each other's availability first because we've already reserved the date. Likewise, if one of us is asked to do something else on that date we know to say 'no' right away because the likelihood of a fireside is very high.

Laura also stresses the importance of recognizing the teaching opportunities we experience all day long.

> We are often teaching without even knowing it. I attend monthly meetings of my professional association and I'm the only Bahá'í there. The others know I'm a Bahá'í and they attribute some of my attitudes during the meetings to my being a Bahá'í, such as the way I stress not talking at the same time when its my turn to chair. Teaching the Faith is about integration. Teaching isn't something I only do at firesides. I am always a Bahá'í, therefore it is integrated into all that I do.

Now look at each of your 'to be' items and break them down into measurable, achievable portions. Put them into time lines, revealing what you need 'to do' each year, month or week, in order to bring your dreams into reality.

This will take some time, so don't rush through it. This is the rest of your life you're planning here! When you're done, I'll meet you in the next chapter, where we will explore how to most effectively use our time on a daily basis.

4
Daily Planning

Dost thou love life?
Then do not squander time,
for that is the stuff life is made of.
Benjamin Franklin

Daily 'To Do' Lists

Making a 'To Do' list isn't corny. It is a sensible tool used by top managers and successful people everywhere. Something that is written down does not have to be mentally reviewed throughout the day, as you try not to forget it. Too often at the end of the day people say, 'Oh, I forgot to do that!' Keeping a 'To Do' list in your head is unreliable and inefficient. Use your mental energy to get your tasks done creatively, not to review *what* you must do.

Many advisors recommend writing your 'To Do' list the evening before. You can plan for tomorrow with the wisdom freshly gleaned from today. You rise in the morning to your list already prepared and can simply begin. While planning for tomorrow you can also ask yourself, 'What kind of person was I today? Did my thoughts, words and actions represent the virtues I am working on?'

If you are a morning person and prefer to plan when you get up, that's fine. After prayer and meditation, and perhaps a cup of coffee, you might be in your best mental condition for planning. I don't think it matters whether you plan in the morning or the evening, just as long as you plan. As the adage says, 'People don't plan to fail, they just fail to plan.'

Your daily 'To Do' lists can be kept in a ring binder notebook. Always siding with simplicity, I use one notebook for everything – taking messages, deepening notes, 'To Do' lists, etc. The removable pages make moving pages, discarding or filing them easy. You could choose a professionally produced personal organizer, popular amongst business people. Several good ones are available at office supply stores. But some of them are so thorough that their large size makes them impractical for many people to carry. If you're not the type to carry a briefcase, you would likely leave your big planning book at home. I prefer to have one all-purpose lightweight notebook and a small calendar in my purse.

Your Notebook or Personal Organizer

Your notebook or organizer is to be used for taking notes throughout the day – as you're jotting down messages and phone numbers from your answering machine, for example. If all such messages are kept in the same book, you will always know where to find them. Directions to someone's house, the name of a book you want to buy and so on can all be recorded in this one trusty notebook.

This notebook is not to be left beside your home phone or on your desk at work. Keep it with you throughout the day to jot down information as it comes to you. If you walk past a house for sale and you are interested, write the realtor's name and phone number down in your book. That notation will always be easier to find than looking for a phone number written on the corner of an envelope at the bottom of your purse.

You might have the type of profession that makes it impractical to have your day-planner with you at all times. If you take it with you in a carry bag you can update your calendar and make notes to yourself during meal and coffee breaks. If this is not practical for you, at least keep a small notepad in your pocket, to write down self-reminders. Leaving something to memory risks losing the information. If you are ever caught without your notebook on you, phone yourself. Yes, phone home and talk to your own answering machine! Leave yourself a message with the information you don't want to forget. You can write it in the correct place once you get home.

Your notebook is also the place to record people's names. Many people say, 'I'm not good at remembering names.' You're normal. So write names down. I keep names in groups in my book – neighbours, Bahá'í friends, work colleagues. If you only see your neighbour once a month it is understandable if you don't recall the person's name easily. It feels good to both you and the other person if you can call him by name. If the name is in your notebook, you'll be able to refresh your memory whenever you need to.

Daily planners sold at bookstores are created for busy professionals, primarily to keep their business lives on schedule. The majority of people, however, do not need a day-planner to organize their work time. They are sales clerks, bus drivers and lab technicians who perform their jobs very well without written plans. When they get *home* is when they need help! No matter what you do for a living, you always come home to a personal life, so keep it together in your own notebook or personal planner.

More and more people are going paperless, using hand-held computers like Palm Pilot® for all of their daily organizing. The thought of having my phone book, 'To Do' lists, a dictionary, road maps and other resources all in one little gadget that fits into my pocket sounds very appealing to me and I'm likely to join soon the ranks of Palm Pilot® users. One could argue which method is best but, truthfully, I believe the best organizer is the one you *will use*. So pick the method you believe will work best in your life and vow to put it into action.

If you do not make 'To Do' lists in a notebook, consider the subtle mental stress you are creating for yourself. Post-it® Notes stuck everywhere do not a 'To Do' list make! They are mentally fatiguing visual clutter. Seeing Post-it® Notes on your desk, wall and fridge causes you to think about undone tasks when you should be giving your full attention to accomplishing something else. A note that says 'Find two chaperones for children's summer school week' interrupts you every time you look at it. In fact, you worry about this item hanging over your head. Instead of using a Post-it® Note, this item should be written onto a 'To Do' list for a specific day, such as next Monday. You don't need to be frequently nagged by thoughts of 'Oh, right, I have to find those chaperones soon'. Rather, on Monday you simply do it.

Post-it® Notes stuck everywhere do not a
'To Do' list make!

Urgent vs. Important

The most important thing *is to remember what things are most important.*

The greatest pitfall people make when deciding how to schedule their time is by not properly distinguishing between urgent and important matters. Urgent items demand our immediate attention. The phone rings; you answer it. Your boss asks you to find something; you drop what you're doing to find it.

Any one of us would agree that our loved ones are more important than our jobs. Yet many parents have spent disproportionate numbers of hours in the workplace, vowing they will spend more time with their families 'soon'. Your boss demanding that a report be ready by tomorrow feels urgent. The opportunity to close more sales today and thereby earn more money is enticingly urgent.

Why are our families never urgent? *Because we assume they will always be there.* Say 'no' to your boss and he may fire you. Say 'sorry, not today' to your son and he will still be your son tomorrow. Yet the same person would say that his child is more important to him than his job. How can this be so? Some workaholics have discovered how urgently they want to be with their families only after their spouses and children have left them. Coming home to an empty house and a goodbye note is an urgent wake-up call.

Suppose 'I want to be a good father' is on your 'To Be' list. How does this translate into an item on your daily 'To Do' list? You schedule in time for your children. By putting this on your list you are making a written commitment to your kids. When you put your son's soccer games on your calendar you are protecting that time with him. If an 'urgent' yet not truly important issue (according to your 'To Be's) wants that same time slot, it is just not available. The alleged urgent item will find another solution and you will have a happy child who knows he is loved.

There are many important things in life that don't feel particularly urgent. Having an annual Pap smear test (even though it might save your life) or writing your will (though it would protect your loved ones should you meet an untimely death) can be repeatedly post-poned with no immediate negative consequences. We can regret how we procrastinated after the bad news comes or we can look at our 'To Be's and live by them. Seeing 'To be healthy' and 'To be a good parent' on a written list reminds us to make the doctor's appoint-ment and write the will.

Urgent items scream loudest for our attention and usually get it. The phone rings, your income tax return is due today, a friend has an urgent request. Meanwhile, the most important parts of our lives – relationships, spiritual development, personal purpose – take a back seat while we put out little fires on a daily basis. By rec-ognizing the difference between urgent and important, and intentionally scheduling time for important things in our lives, we feel better at day's end about how we spent our time.

This does not mean the urgent things will go away. As long as you are sharing this planet with other people, there will always be so-called urgent items people place in your path. Your 'To Do' list will always have items on it that are not crossed off. The difference that occurs when you put the most important things first is that you go to bed feeling good about how you spent your time that day. The undone items lose their significance when you have given time to the items that matter most in your life.

Additional Tips

Assign your tasks according to your energy cycles. Give your most important items your best time. Are you at your brightest in the mornings? Write that speech first thing after breakfast. Leave other duties, like doing laundry, until the evening when you are your least creative and can run on auto-pilot.

Look at your list frequently throughout the day, to ensure you have not drifted off course. Being busy all day can still leave you feeling unfulfilled if you did the wrong things.

Schedule dates with your spouse and mark them on your calendar. Guard those time slots with all that is holy.

If you have several phone calls to make, it is more efficient to sit down and do them all together.

Keep all your notes to yourself in your notebook (or hand-held computer). Whether phoning for estimates to have your house painted or jotting down the flight number of someone you're picking up at the airport, you will please yourself to have all your information in one place where you can find it again.

During phone calls, write down the names of people you speak to and when you spoke with them. If there is a dispute later, you can say impressive things like 'I made the reservation with Richard on 10 April at 9:00 a.m.' That kind of credibility goes a long way when resolving a conflict.

> A man who dares to waste one hour of his life
> has not discovered the value of life.
> *Charles Darwin*

5

Creating Balance

Living a balanced life does not mean the same thing to all people. If everyone prayed, taught the Faith, worked, shopped and slept the same amount of time as everyone else, life would be far less interesting. Each person chooses his own right mix. A single person's day is going to look quite different from that of a mother of three but both can be living a balanced life.

Finding balance can be a struggle. So many demands want our time. Life comes at us in continual waves and the water never seems to calm. In order to experience peace and balance in a busy world, it is essential first to understand that the waves are not the enemy. Life and time are not conspiring against us.

Being 'on top of things' doesn't mean you've reached your goals, there are no dishes in the sink and the 'in' basket on your desk is empty. *Everything is never 'caught up' in life.* Being happy cannot be postponed until all life's chores are done and your ambitions are achieved because that moment will never arrive. Something always wants doing. Happiness is experienced when a person asks, 'How much can I reasonably expect of myself today?' Then he takes pleasure in doing those things, *without* feeling mentally burdened by what he didn't do.

When we accept the waves in life as natural and necessary, we no longer feel victimized by them. Balance in life requires continual reassessment and repositioning. Stand up on your surfboard and enjoy the ride! It's the waves in your life that make it interesting. Shoghi Effendi stated:

> The Bahá'ís, in spite of their self-sacrificing desire to give the last drop of their strength to serving the Cause, must guard against utterly depleting their forces and having breakdowns. For this can sometimes do more harm than good, because they are so bound up in the lives of others . . .
>
> There is no doubt that there is vicarious atonement for others, and our sufferings sometimes can be in the nature of a sacrifice accepted for others. But where to draw the line is a mystery. *If you take better care of your own health, and build up your reserves, it would certainly be better for you and for your work.* Then your sensitive, yearning heart, although you may still often suffer for and with others, will be better able to withstand its trials, and you will not get so exhausted, which is certainly no asset to your work for the Cause.[1]

The following are several strategies to help busy Bahá'ís find the balance they long for.

Saying 'No'

We have many time-saving devices in our society, but . . .

> *The best time-saving device is the word 'No'.*

Saying 'no' is painfully hard for many Bahá'ís. To say 'no' when asked to be involved in something makes a lot of us feel uneasy. It's easier to say 'yes' to something you don't want to do or haven't really got time for than to say an outright 'no' to someone.

To be chronically unable to say 'no' when you clearly should has been coined 'the disease to please'. Some people fear rejection or hurting another person so much they go too far in their desire to please others. It is a self-esteem problem and may require professional help.

There are ways to recognize when you can say 'yes' and how to say a graceful, guilt-free 'no' when it is necessary. The goal is to feel good when you say 'yes' as well as when you say 'no'.

When you have a clearly written 'To Be' list, knowing when to say 'yes' and when to say 'no' is so much easier. If something supports who you want to be, then bring it on. If accepting a new request means you will neglect important 'To Be's, then don't do it. With 'I want to be a loyal servant of Bahá'u'lláh' on their 'To Be' lists, some Bahá'ís feel an obligation to accept all the opportunities to serve that come along. But consider this: if 'I want to be a parent' is on your list, is this an obligation to have 24 children? Of course not. Balance is required in all that we do, including service to the Bahá'í Faith.

When a Bahá'í friend offers you an opportunity to serve, and you're uncertain whether or not you should say an immediate 'yes', consider responding in the following way: 'Thank you for asking me. I will pray about it and get back to you.' No one can object to such a responsible method of decision-making!

If after prayer and meditation you are still not one hundred per cent certain how to respond, remember that almighty word 'consultation'. Call a trusted friend to help you work out the issue. We are encouraged to consult with others on matters large and small.

Also remember to consult your own 'To Be' list. If you can honour the request and still attend to the priority items of who you want to be, then by all means be generous with your time. But if there is a conflict, stay true to who you aspire to be.

Your gut feelings are highly reliable. When a request comes your way, you usually get an instantaneous yes/no sensation inside. What you say in response, however, might contradict that instinct. Before saying 'yes' to something because that's the easiest way to handle the moment, first ask yourself, 'What are the consequences of *not* saying no?' If you answer, 'I will have no evenings with my kids for two weeks' and that feels wrong to you, then 'no' is the best answer.

Trying to inch out of the conversation by saying 'maybe' is unfair to both parties. The other person remains hopeful that you will later confirm your involvement. You also have set yourself up to relive the request, for that person will come back to you and ask all over again. Get it over with. If 'no' is going to be the answer, then say it now.

There are ways you can still be helpful if you must decline the original request. Tell the person what you *are* able to offer. 'No, I'm sorry I cannot be the chairperson for that function but I *can* do the calligraphy for the posters.'

We all have close friends with whom we can honestly say, 'You know, I just don't feel up to doing that' and they will respect our decision. With people with whom you are not so close, *do not feel obliged to always explain why you cannot do something.* To truthfully say, 'Sorry, I'll be out of town that day' is a fortunate and easy way out. You are conveniently and understandably excused. But what if the subject just doesn't interest you and you don't feel comfortable bluntly saying so? You might be tempted to say things like 'I'd love to help on the project but I don't have a fax machine' or 'I don't have a babysitter that day'. When you do this, the other party might start problem-solving for you. She just might have a spare fax machine or a 15-year-old daughter who's looking for more babysitting jobs. Then you're stuck with the task, all because you tried to use an excuse.

Don't be caught making excuses. If you could help with the project but you are not willing to drop your other priorities to do it, the best response is, 'Thank you for asking me, but I'm just not available to help with that.' There might be a brief pause from the other person (because people are accustomed to hearing excuses) but you don't have to pretend you have another engagement. If you said you are not available, then you are not available. A well-mannered person is not going to pry with 'Why?'

Not offering an explanation for saying 'no' is also appropriate when you feel that to give the honest reason would:

- not be understood by the listener
- be met with judgement by the listener or
- hurt the listener's feelings

Don't be caught making excuses

Once you have said 'no' and you know it is the right response, you begin to feel better almost immediately. There are the initial pangs of disappointment for not being able to do all you want for someone else but those pangs quickly pass when you know you have given the best answer – unlike the pain of being burdened with a task you originally knew you should not have taken on.

In the quest for having balance in her life, Jennifer, a secretary in a new job, decided that saying 'no' was something she needed to implement at work. Her boss was often asking her to work late on short notice. 'You don't mind staying late to finish this up, do you?' her boss would say, leaving files on her desk, walking away without waiting for a response. It was assumed that Jennifer would stay.

One day Jennifer finally said, 'Sorry, no, I can't stay today.' Without offering an excuse, Jennifer handed the file back to her boss and carried on with her work. She knew the risk involved. If not staying late meant she could get fired, Jennifer had decided ahead of time that she would accept those consequences.

'But I need you to stay!' said the boss.

'When you hired me I was told I would work until 5:30 each day.' Jennifer answered. 'I've given you eight hours of quality work today and now I need to go home to my daughter.'

The boss stayed late and finished the work himself. After all, he did own the business. Jennifer is a hard worker and her boss recognized that and wanted to keep her. Jennifer still works at the same office. She stays late once in a while but not as a general rule. She has chosen her family as a priority. As much as she also needs a job, Jennifer has decided that, for her, 40 hours a week is all her job is getting of her time.

Once your priorities are clear, living with the consequences of guarding them is easier to take, even when a few losses are involved.

'I don't think Bahá'ís have trouble saying "no",' a man said during a time management seminar I was presenting. 'I have trouble finding people to say "yes" and help with things!'

'The title of this seminar is *Time and Life Management for Busy Bahá'ís*,' I replied. 'How to motivate less-involved Bahá'ís is not my area of expertise. How over-extended Bahá'ís can regain balance is something I do know about. Have you heard about the 80/20 Rule?' I asked him. He hadn't.

The 80/20 Rule

Vilfredo Pareto was a 19th century Italian economist and sociologist who noted cases in which a small percentage of people within a society account for a much larger percentage of a particular trait attributed to that society. Pareto's Law is commonly referred to as the '80/20 Rule'.

Pareto's Law still holds true in its application to numerous social and economic scenarios today. In sales, roughly 80 per cent of a company's business is done with 20 per cent of its customers. In a group, 20 per cent of the people will often do 80 per cent of the talking (hopefully not during Bahá'í consultation!). Eighty per cent of a company's sick time is taken by 20 per cent of its employees. Eighty per cent of the fat you ingest is contained in 20 per cent of the food you eat. Eighty per cent of the disruptions during class time are caused by 20 per cent of the students. You get the picture.

One implication in Bahá'í life is that 80 per cent of an Assembly's time is taken up by 20 per cent of its agenda. If you are an Assembly member, you can attest that this is agonizingly true. Sensitive personal matters cannot be hurried over and may take a seemingly disproportionate amount of time. If a community member is puzzled by how 'slow' the Assembly appears to be in responding to some presumably simple matters, it is often due to the serious nature of a mere few other agenda items.

For the Bahá'í at the seminar who found more people saying 'no' to his invitations for service than those who would say 'yes', the 80/20 Rule was at play. 80 per cent of the volunteer work is often done by a dedicated 20 per cent of the Bahá'ís.

While the Pareto Principle is not exact, it does give you a historic meter by which to gauge how you should be spending your time. Twenty per cent of your 'To Do' list will require 80 per cent of your time. This is why choosing priorities is so vital. The less important items might not get touched at all. When planning your day, the goal is not to complete the greatest number of items possible from your 'To Do' list. *The goal is to do the most important ones.*

In teaching the Faith, 20 per cent of your contacts will get 80 per cent of your attention. They are the most receptive. The majority of your firesides will be with the seekers who are most keen.

Twenty percent of your home gets 80 per cent of the cleaning attention and rightfully so. High traffic areas such as the kitchen and bathroom need more frequent cleaning than basements and bedrooms.

Think of other ways the 80/20 rule applies to your life. Then let this dictate how you distribute your most valuable resource – your time.

Hurry

> There is more to life than increasing its speed.
> *Gandhi*

Why is our culture so fascinated with hurrying? For many people, being in a rush is simply an acquired habit. 'I'm always running late!' they say. Hurry sickness has even made its way into the lyrics of popular music:

> I'm in a hurry to get things done
> Oh I rush and rush until life's no fun
> All I really gotta do is live and die
> But I'm in a hurry and don't know why.
> *(from 'I'm in a Hurry', by Alabama, American Pride CD, RCA, 1992)*

Once upon a time you were not in a hurry. You used to be a peaceful baby, thriving on milk and cuddles. Remember your childhood and youth, when life seemed so much simpler? You played and went to school. Somewhere between then and now you became a harried adult, with a faster life and higher stress level. Yes, you have more serious responsibilities now and I don't suggest you abandon them. But the point is that nearly all the things that make you feel too busy nowadays are things you voluntarily brought into your life.

Though you may feel you have signed up for more than you can handle at times, the fact remains that you are still in the driver's seat of your life and you *can* regain control of its speed.

How many times in a day do you hurry? When you get ready for work, do you eat breakfast, shower and dress with a little more haste than you wish? Do you increase your walking speed, even run, to catch a light at a street corner? Do you step on the gas in the hope of going through a yellow light? Do you talk faster to a work colleague when trying to meet a deadline? Do you ever walk faster, indoors or out, because you think you need to get somewhere sooner? Do you ever say to yourself, 'I'm going to be late'? Do you apologize at meetings or work for arriving late?

Hurry is a part of western lifestyle. I applaud anyone from a different culture who can read the above paragraph and ask, 'What is she talking about?' Such folk are usually happier and healthier than their hurried counterparts. But back to us and the hurry sickness that plagues our culture and erodes our spiritual development.

Modern inventions like the washing machine and vacuum cleaner were marketed to us as convenience items, destined to make our lives easier. Machines would do our tedious work and leave us with more leisure time. Despite all the alleged time-saving inventions created by man, we are now busier than ever.

But did you know: Hurry is a choice. You can be part of it or you can simply opt out. You can choose not to be a hurried person.

Busy vs. Hurry

Let's first differentiate between being busy and being in a hurry. Being busy does not necessarily mean you are hurrying. Busy just means you are a person in motion with tasks to do. You can be involved with many things yet focus only on one item at a time and not feel overwhelmed. Nor do you hurry.

Let's ask ourselves whether the Master, 'Abdu'l-Bahá, would choose to be a hurried person. If He were alive today, try to imagine at what speed He would go about His daily affairs. Do you see 'Abdu'l-Bahá getting dressed as fast as He can, skipping His morning prayers because He slept in? Would He run up the stairs, two at a time, trying to catch the phone on the second ring? I think not.

I imagine the Master moving through each day with *gentle efficiency*. No running, no yelling, no panicking. He would start each day with prayer and meditation. He would go forth about His work at a sensible and efficient pace.

Martin Luther King said that when he woke up and thought that his day was too busy to start with prayer, those were the days when he knew that he absolutely must pray first.

The High Price of Hurry

If you frequently hurry, you are not getting away with it. Something in your life is paying the price. Usually it's your health or your serenity. Your body lovingly gives you clues when it needs you to slow down. You might get a cold or feel fatigued. If you don't listen to its pleas, it will speak louder to you. If you still don't listen, its cry for rest will get louder still.

'I have absolutely no doubt that when I slipped on the stairs and broke my ankle it was a clear message that I had to slow down,' one Bahá'í revealed. 'Suddenly all the things I thought I *had* to do I could not do. I couldn't even drive my car. I was forced to rest. At first I was anxious about all the things I had to get done, but I humbly realized that I was not indispensable after all. The world continued to function without me. I actually began to appreciate the time at home and took a good hard look at how I was conducting my life. I'm glad I got the message with my broken ankle. I wouldn't want a larger warning signal like a tumour or major accident.'

Learning to Slow Down

Here is your assignment: Go through one full day without any hurry. Get up ten minutes earlier to get ready for the day without rushing. If you're going to miss the bus unless you run, just miss it. There will be another one. Do not step on the gas to get through a traffic light, just stop the car at the red light and enjoy the view. At work do not run to catch an elevator; take the next one. Purposely go for a walk on a busy street to practise the art of not hurrying by not running to catch a cross light. Walk to answer the phone; if you miss the call, delight in one less interruption. Give yourself enough time to prepare a meal so that you do nothing hurriedly; just enjoy putting love into your creation.

Do you recognize some of these examples as your own common moments of hurry? At what other times do you rush? You were not created to hurry. As you go about a day designated as 'No Hurry Day' you will astonish yourself – first, by how often you need to slow yourself down; second, by how good the gentle pace feels! You will breathe more deeply, smile more and be more aware of your surroundings. You will be a better listener to the people around you. You will be more aware of your own boundaries and know when it is the right time to say 'no' to something. Serenity will be your reward. Try it for one full day. If you like it, go for another day. If serenity is not for you, you can always go back to rushing.

Three years ago I applied a 'Walk Don't Run' approach to my whole life. I liked it so much I'm still doing it and will forever more. Its impact on my spiritual, mental and physical health has been nothing short of profound.

> Whoever is in a hurry
> shows that the thing he is about
> is too big for him.
> *Lord Chesterfield*

Enough is Enough

> Have no fear of perfection – you'll never reach it.
> *Salvador Dali*

Are you able to recognize when you have done enough? When doing a task we are not particularly fond of, such as cleaning the bathroom, it is not too difficult to say, 'That's good enough', and move on to another task or even take a nap. Yet we humans tend to fritter away minute after minute (which add up to hours a week) on tasks we resist acknowledging as complete.

My weakness is with writing. No writing project is small; they are all works of art, if only in my own mind. If I am writing a simple card to a friend, I will first write the passage on a scrap of paper, scratch out words, draw arrows. I will eventually, and ever so carefully, transcribe the final masterpiece onto the card. If I think I have written a particularly brilliant piece of prose I will read and reread the card, admiring my own work, imagining how the recipient of the card will feel. (I'm also this laborious with gift-wrapping!) The recipient of the card, however, will read it in a matter of seconds and likely disregard how well balanced each line is set on the card or admire my amateur calligraphy. An event that should take me two minutes to complete takes me 15! With those 13 extra minutes I could tidy my desk or my kitchen.

We all have things we linger over, when saying 'This is enough' would be wiser. Consider the student who spends 12 consecutive hours researching a paper, where the last two hours produce little value compared to the first ten. If he would stop at hour ten and say, 'This is plenty good' he would have the benefit of two more hours of much needed sleep. (Incidentally, the more you research something, the greater the possibility of finding conflicting information. Then you've really created more work for yourself!)

Or the woman who spends ten extra minutes in the morning trying to make her hair do something it doesn't want to do and she leaves the house looking no better than if she hadn't fought with her hair. Or the hours spent comparison shopping when the item you end up buying was at the first store you went to (and your instincts tried to tell you to buy it then and be done with it but you wouldn't listen!).

We waste time talking too long on the telephone when the conversation could be wrapped up earlier. Some people clean excessively. Others eat. Many folks are still sitting in front of the television long after their programme is over.

Parkinson's Law states that 'work will expand or contract to fill the time available'. So don't over-budget precious time for a task when less time will get the same results. Look for opportunities where you can say 'This is enough' and you will discover several minutes a day, hours a week, to devote to the things you thought you had no time for.

Punctuality

> I've been on a calendar
> but I've never been on time!
> *Marilyn Monroe*

If someone says, 'Oh, we're running on Bahá'í time!' what does that mean to you? Unfortunately most readers will say, 'That means things are running late.' It's a shame that so many Bahá'ís use and recognize that expression! It's often followed by a giggle, as if 'Bahá'í time' were so cute and acceptable.

It's not cute and it's not acceptable. And you certainly won't find that term in the Bahá'í writings. Wipe that phrase out of your vocabulary if you use it. And please don't give an approving smile when another Bahá'í uses that term. Making 'Bahá'í time' synonymous with being late dishonours the reputation of the Faith.

Unfaithfulness in the keeping of an appointment
is an act of clear dishonesty.
You may as well borrow a person's money as his time.
Horace Mann

Repeated tardiness is a rehearsed behaviour. It *can* be overcome if a person is willing. People don't miss airline flights when they have paid a few thousand dollars for their vacations. Some people who are routinely late for work or for Feasts will be at their airplanes on time. The ability to be punctual is equal for all our affairs, depending on how much respect we have for them. A number of virtues are being snubbed when we are late, including courtesy and respect. This is true whether a person walks into Feast late or is not on time to meet someone for lunch (flat tyres and medical emergencies excluded). It is a display of disrespect to others any time we are late.

When the organizers of an event do not start on time, it is disrespectful to all the people who *do* show up on time. It also conditions people to arrive late next time because 'these things never start on time'. If you are hosting an event, start at the advertised hour. It is appreciated and expected by the people who are present on time. As for those who do arrive late, you are helping them by setting an example of punctuality. Holding the show for latecomers only reinforces tardiness and is not in line with virtuous behaviour.

I would rather be an hour early
than a minute late.
Patricia Williams, my grandmother

6

Organizing Your Home

Everybody has a home life. No matter how many books you read on time management for the office or how to be a better manager at work, you still have to come home. Your laundry, your kids, your rubbish and your clutter are all there waiting for you. This practical chapter addresses effective time management on the home front.

'I can organize the world but I can't organize myself!' Is this you? Do you do well at managing a project at work or for a Bahá'í committee but feel your personal life is disorganized? It *is* possible to get your personal life in order too.

'Abdu'l-Bahá has told us that 'The home should be orderly and well-organized.'[1] Besides getting organized just because it makes good sense to you, realize that you are also obeying the Master.

The smallest of chores can take up inordinate amounts of conscious thought if they persistently remain undone. They nag at you. 'Look at me! I'm still here! Mess to tidy up!' While you try to focus on another task, or even try to rest, the guilt from the 'undone' spoils the quality of that time.

A LOT can be accomplished in a few minutes. You do not have to wait until you have 20 minutes to clean the

whole bathroom. Just wipe the sink and counter. It will look shiny clean and you feel better until you have the 20 minutes another day. Got five minutes before your car-pool ride arrives? Two minutes during television ads? Give yourself the gratification of a noticeable task done. The following are examples of tasks that can be accomplished in one to ten minutes:

- Take out the rubbish
- Spot dust the living room
- Have a race with your child to see who can put away the most toys
- Load or unload the dishwasher
- Pick the laundry off the bedroom floor and put it in the basket

- Tidy the shoe/boot area at the door
- Clean a mirror
- Water the plants
- Sort the junk from your purse, briefcase or gym bag

Look around your home and identify the multitude of quick jobs that can be done. Five minutes of tidying goes a long way! It not only cleans part of your home but it's a gift to your sanity. You feel better about the state of your home.

Want to watch TV? Iron a few items of clothing at the same time. You'll be thankful one day when you are dressing hurriedly and find your shirt already ironed. Do your manicure while you watch TV. Sew on a button. Do a few sit-ups or stretching exercises.

Clutter

> Out of clutter, find simplicity.
> *Albert Einstein*

Evaluate where your clutter comes from. Ask yourself, 'Why do I keep such things?' If you tend to keep things because they might become useful someday, remember this: *everything*, if saved long enough, will eventually have a use someday! But ask yourself, do you really need to keep the old toaster in case the new one breaks down someday? Do you really need to keep all your maternity clothes in case your younger sister gets married, and eventually pregnant, *someday*?

When struggling with 'Should I throw it out or not?', ask yourself, 'Could I possibly get this item again if I needed to in the future?' If the answer is 'yes' (and it nearly always is), let it go. Recycle, sell, donate or trash it. You don't need to hang on to everything 'just in case'. Most paper information items are easily replaceable – highway maps for places you seldom go to, brochures, etc. If you're keeping a pair of size 6 trousers in case you lose 50 pounds someday, give them away. If you lose the weight, you deserve a new pair of trousers!

The state of tidiness of your home (or purse/wallet/car) reflects your state of mind. A disorganized home suggests cluttered mental organization. There is no room for peace of mind when the *space* your mind lives in is overcrowded. On the days when your personal living space is orderly, notice how you feel more peaceful and on top of matters in general. A stressed-out friend said, 'I'm not disorganized, I'm just in a hurry. Because I'm involved in so many things, my home gets a little messy, that's all.'

My friend was confusing being busy with being organized. The mess at home was telling a tale on her. She takes on a lot and keeps up the appearance of being on top of it all. The mess says about her, 'I'm actually overwhelmed and losing control'. But if she took the few extra *seconds* required to put things in their places as she went along, she truly would be on top of her life. She could be busy and have peace of mind too.

Stored Stuff

Sometimes the thought of sorting through boxes of stored possessions in the garage, basement or closet feels much too ominous. Yet you'd love to have the feeling of knowing it all got dealt with somehow. Take this strategy: sit down with one box of 'stuff' and give yourself a time limit, such as 'I'm going to throw away as much of this stuff in ten minutes as I can'. That means you don't linger re-reading old letters. You don't reminisce and try on old clothes. You definitely don't say, 'Maybe this will come in useful some day.' Throw it out! After the ten minutes is up, decide if you want to go for another ten or pat yourself on the back for the amount you did accomplish and put the box back.

The things we keep in boxes are more of sentimental value than useful, otherwise we would be using them. Only keep the good photographs when you get them developed, rather than putting the whole set into a photo box that grows and grows until you dread having to sort through it all one day.

Moving into a new home often reveals to people what they need and what they don't. If a box of stuff goes unpacked for a few months, maybe you don't need the contents at all. After her sixth move, a good friend finally admitted she didn't need to keep the boxes of lecture notes and essays she had been carrying around since her university days. She disposed of them all.

Motivational speaker Caroline Baxter has admirable courage. One day while looking for something in her basement she came across three boxes that were unopened since her last move. She couldn't remember what was inside them. 'If I haven't opened these boxes in three years then I obviously don't need whatever is in there,' she said to herself. So she threw all three of them out – unopened!

I once met a couple the wife of which loved to shop. She really didn't need more clothing; she just had trouble resisting a dress sale. It became a contentious issue in their marriage. They did find a creative solution, though. Her husband said he would stop complaining or starting arguments about her purchases if she would please follow a simple rule: 'If you buy *one*, you throw out *two*.' Whether it's a dress or a pair of socks, if she buys one, she gets rid of two. For someone who enjoys shopping just for fashion's sake, it's a good way to keep the closets from becoming overcrowded.

Divergent Thinking

Time management experts advise you do only one thing at a time. If you're cleaning out the fridge, then just clean the fridge. Don't start cleaning other areas of the kitchen until you are done with the fridge. It makes sense, I agree, but I just can't seem to do it. I have the attention span of a puppy. Witness me cleaning house: I'll go to the bedroom to put a sweater away in the closet. In the bedroom I encounter a pile of clean laundry on the bed so I start to fold. After folding the tea towels I put them away in the kitchen where I discover dishes on the counter and put them into the dishwasher. I then take out the kitchen rubbish. Walking back inside I see a pair of shoes in the doorway that goes back to the bedroom. In the bedroom the remainder of the laundry awaits me and I finish folding. Thirty to 60 minutes will pass while I circle about my home, cleaning and putting things away, naughtily disobeying the time management gurus.

Then I read *Time Management for Unmanageable People* by Ann McGee-Cooper and Duane Trammell. Hallelujah, I'm normal! They call it divergent think-ing. Divergent thinkers juggle several balls at once. That's just how their brains are wired and it works for them. As I'm writing this chapter, all the other chapters of this book are also three-quarters written. When I'm having difficulty with a paragraph in one chapter I might be struck with an idea for another chapter and I switch to that computer file for a while. I might work on three different chapters in one day. The mere fact that you are now holding onto this book is testament that my divergent methods still resulted in a finished manuscript.

There are times when even the divergent thinker must focus, however, such as when writing a speech. To get up and start fluffing pillows before you've written a word is procrastination, not endearing divergence. If you are a divergent thinker trying to write a speech, sit down and write for a set time period, say 20 minutes.

When the time is up, ask yourself if you can do another 15 minutes. If not, schedule another 20 minute period for later that day or the day after. Your speech *will* be written on time if you commit to it in realistic doses.

People who can focus on one task for longer periods of time are called convergent thinkers. I don't believe one way of thinking is better than the other, any more than being right- or left-handed could be right or wrong. You just are who you are. You could even be a mixture of both types. I find it easy to be convergent when in meetings and sticking to the agenda while, as you already know, I'm divergent when cleaning my home. Recognize which kind of thinker you are and make the best of your skills. If you have divergent traits, now you know there is nothing wrong with you, if you still get the job done.

Granddad's Put-It-Back

If getting your life organized seems an impossibly big task right now, here is one simple deed that will make an astonishing difference in your life: 'If you use something . . . put it back.' Sounds too easy, doesn't it? Yet so many of us don't do it. It feels easier at the time to just leave the scissors on the coffee table or throw a jacket over a chair but it is not easier, *just lazier*. Not putting things away creates more work. Plus there is mental stress when you look at the clutter. Most clutter is stuff that doesn't need to be where it is simply because someone couldn't be bothered to put something back immediately after using it. Often a few seconds is all that is required. By taking a few steps to put something where it belongs when you're done with it goes a very long way to reducing clutter in your home. So next time you're about to leave a cup on an end table or drop your socks on the floor, as a gift to yourself take five seconds to put them in their places. The tidiness will soothe you.

After my mother passed away my two sisters and I met at her house to sort her belongings. We three women sat on the living room carpet going over small sentimental items, while our husbands were in the background moving furniture. Our conversation as overheard by the men went like this:

'Do you want Granddad's Put-It-Back?'

'It would be nice, but I have my own Put-It-Back now. Do you need Granddad's Put-It-Back?'

'I'd love it! I don't have a Put-It-Back. I would love to have Granddad's Put-It-Back.'

The men stopped what they were doing and stared at each other, confirming that our conversation didn't make sense to any of them. One of them sighed and spoke for the group.

'What on earth is a "Put-It-Back"?' he asked.

'This!' exclaimed one sister, holding a metal measuring tape high over her head.

You see, our mother cherished the tape measure that had once belonged to her father. He had long since passed away and this was one of the few items of his that she still had. During our younger years at home, whenever one of us asked to use the tape measure, Mom would reply, 'Yes, but it's Granddad's, put it back!' It always sounded like one connected phrase. Rather than call it Granddad's tape measure, the item became known in our household as 'Granddad's Put-It-Back'.

We never lost the Put-It-Back because we . . . well, you know . . . always put it back. Imagine how easy it would be to find things in your home if you were always this conscientious with returning your possessions to their places.

The purpose behind putting things back is twofold. First, you have prevented clutter. And second, you have saved time. Add up the minutes you spend each week looking for things and it amounts to too much time. Make this your motto: If it takes more than 30 seconds to find something, it's in the wrong place!

Imagine if you spent one hour a week simply looking for things that were not in their places. That is a conservative figure, as most people consume much more time, yes, waste time, over the course of a week performing the completely preventable task of searching for an object not returned to its designated spot. Five minutes searching for keys, ten minutes paper-digging for a lost item on your desk . . . it adds up.

That conservative hour a week translates into 52 hours a year! Why, that's enough time to read several good books, exercise off a few pounds, write and mail 52 letters, always have a clean bathroom, take 52 good naps or have 52 quality conversations with a significant other. What would you like to do with 52 'bonus' hours a year? Keeping things simple and organized is essential to your quality of life. Ongoing clutter prevention and putting things back saves you hours of frustration. Our grandmothers were right: 'A place for everything and everything in its place.'

Getting Your Family On-side

Turning a new leaf and becoming a person who manages her time and life better is rewarding for you. If you live with others, though, your transformation might get a cool reception. If you decide that it's wise to wipe the bathroom taps after every use and reduce the frequency of major cleanings, this will require cooperation from the rest of your family. Unfortunately, they are not likely to embrace your new strategies with your same exuberance because they haven't been through your metamorphosis.

To get your family on-side, have a family meeting. Tell them why you need to change your habits for yourself and that you need their support. Paint an enticing picture for them of how your household could operate for the better. Show them what's in it for them. Ask your spouse to read this book. Share with your loved ones the most important changes you hope the family can make together, whether it's wiping taps or having everyone get up ten minutes earlier to leave for work and school unrushed. Consult together. Let everyone give his point of view. Then make a decision together. If your spouse and kids feel that they helped form the decision, they are likely to support it.

In the days and weeks to come, bite your tongue if everything is not going as you had hoped. Remember, there is more than one right way to do the same tasks. The other family members might not do the dishes the same way you do or sweep the floor as effectively as you would but let them do it their way, anyway. To criticize now would undermine the ground you have gained. If your family is trying, in any way, to contribute to the changes you suggested, consider it a victory. Hold occasional family meetings to evaluate your progress together and introduce additional improvements gradually.

Additional Tips

Is hand-washable-only laundry piling up on you? Take
one small item, such as an item of lingerie, into the
shower with you and wash it while you shower.

Just because something is free doesn't mean you have to
take it (make-up samples, magazines, etc.). They add
unwanted clutter to your home.

Just because something is on sale or cheaper by the
dozen doesn't mean you need to over-fill your cup-
boards with products you might use someday.

Broken small appliances often cost the same to replace as
repair. Don't store them. Discard them appropriately or
give them to someone who can repair and reuse them.

Avoid grocery shopping at peak hours.

Always put your keys in the same place. A wall-hook
hidden inside your entrance closet is a good location.

Cleaning as you cook leaves a much appreciated
smaller mess after meals.

Choose clothing that requires little upkeep, such as no-
iron trousers. Before buying something that requires
dry-cleaning or hand-washing ask yourself, 'Is it really
worth the fuss?'

Free yourself of unnecessary household items. Some
'collectibles' are really dust collectors.

Think twice before getting a pet. Be certain you will dedicate the time required to care for the pet and that you can accept the unavoidable messes.

Have a chalkboard, corkboard or erasable white board available for family members to leave each other messages.

Do you know where your flashlight, fire extinguisher and other emergency equipment are? Do you know how to use them? Don't wait for a crisis to learn how they work.

Give family members an area of the house where they can each be messy, one shelf or small table for example. This way, if they feel a need to pile things, each person knows his little corner where this is permissible. When the pile gets too high, the owner has to reduce it.

Hang coat hooks at your entranceway so family members can easily hang their coats. Kids are less likely to put them on the floor if a hook is easy to reach. The same also works well in kids' bedrooms.

Is your bathroom counter cluttered with toiletries? Buy an attractive basket and drape a small colourful towel inside. Toss your cosmetics and other personal paraphernalia into this one tidy receptacle.

Gentlemen: want to score really big points with your wives? If you give her a gift of being pampered, ALSO pamper the house. While she is out having a facial and pedicure, clean the house or hire a maid service to do it for you!

Kids seldom notice the disappearance of toys they've outgrown. Thin your child's toy collection for him when he's not around and give the old toys to charity.

Just because something was a gift does not oblige you to keep it. If you receive a gift but it's just not your style, pass it on to someone else who will enjoy it more.

Hire a babysitter *on a day that you're home.* You can organize a room, make phone calls without interruptions, exercise, enjoy a long bath, etc.

Reorganize your household in stages. Remember, it didn't get this disorganized overnight.

7

Your Home Office

The Home Office

A home office is not only for people working out of their homes. Everybody has a home office. Whether it's a separate room in your house or only a corner in your kitchen, you have to keep your bills and important papers somewhere. Everyone's life has a paper flow. Once you get control of your home paper flow amazing things start to happen. You can find things! You are less apt to procrastinate (like at income tax time) if you can easily find what you need. You can focus better on any task when your work space is orderly. When you invest a little time to organize your home office you have more time for the things that matter most to you.

Time management books are often directed at professional managers. Tips such as 'Have your secretary sort and thin your mail before it reaches your desk' are suggested. How nice! Who among us has a secretary doing this for us at home? Everyone has a personal life, no matter what one's professional title may be. Although any of the principles espoused in this book can be implemented in the professional office, this book is directed at how you manage your *personal* time and space. This is a fun chapter. It's about becoming the master of your home office.

'Where Does This Go?'

To test your organized/disorganized status, imagine the following items entering your household via your mailbox or things you carry in. Ask yourself, 'Where will I put this?' Not 'Where *should* it go?' but 'Where would I honestly put it first?' Picture yourself handling these items:

- Your credit card invoice
- A flyer from a new restaurant you'd like to try
- A brochure from a political candidate
- An invoice from your insurance company
- A statement from your retirement investments
- Your child's report card from school
- An Ayyám-i-Há party invitation card for your child
- Notes you took during a special Bahá'í lecture
- Your notes from a Bahá'í committee meeting
- A business card of a new fireside contact
- A page of coupons the grocery clerk put in your grocery bag
- A reminder notice for your next dental check-up
- A magazine you subscribe to
- A notice from the city, changing your rubbish collection days
- A cheque from someone who owed you $50.00
- The daily newspaper that arrives at your doorstep
- A business card from a house painter you might need in a few months

- Photos just developed
- Tickets for an event four weeks away

How many of the above items landed on your kitchen or living room table in the 'I'll deal with it later pile'? It's a common tendency to wish things would go away or wish they'd put themselves away. But they don't. Adding something to a pile on a table is creating a pile of procrastination – things you could have done. Dealing with items as they arrive is the swiftest way to eliminate them. Having the right tools for the job increases the probability that you *will* process your paper flow as you receive it.

Go Shopping

Mastering your home office begins with a shopping trip. Get a catalogue from an office supply store and browse through it. Find items that would help you be more organized on the home front. Determine your budget and go to the store. With a basket or shopping cart, slowly go up and down the aisles and select items that will make your home office space function more smoothly. Having the right tools makes any job easier and more enjoyable. For example, if your home filing system is a collection of shoe boxes, envelopes and paper piles, it's time to upgrade. It's time to buy some proper filing supplies.

The following are suggestions for your shopping spree:

- File folders
- Hanging files

- File boxes or cabinet
- New pens, various colours
- Pencils, sharpener, erasers
- Paper clips
- A desk-top container for the above items
- Adhesive tape
- Post-it® Notes
- Stapler and staples
- Note pads, various sizes
- Envelopes, various sizes
- Stamps
- Scissors
- Calculator
- Hole punch
- Ruler
- Business card file
- Waste paper basket
- Recycling bin

Strolling through the aisles of an office supply store can be intriguing. Manufacturers continue to create colourful new tools and toys to appeal to consumers. Since the paper flow in your home never ceases, it's worth investing in the tools that will help you manage it. If you enjoy the tools you buy, you might even enjoy the work!

Bringing home these new items is very refreshing. It inspires you to keep a tidy desk top. There is one rule however: Before you unpack any of your new office tools, THROW OUT THE OLD ONES! Empty your drawers of any pens that aren't working or that you don't like. Throw out the broken stapler and all the rubber bands cluttering a drawer. Now replenish your desk with your new tools. Tidy up your work area. Put note pads and pens in accessible places.

Furniture

Your shopping trip might include buying office furniture such as a desk or bookshelves. A second-hand desk or computer station is just fine. Bookshelves are a necessity for most anyone who can read. Bahá'ís in particular tend to develop personal libraries of Bahá'í and other literature. Videos and CDs have to go somewhere too.

You will need somewhere to store files. If you can find a filing cabinet for a reasonable price and you have the space to keep a filing cabinet, buy one if you want it. Otherwise, filing boxes are a practical alternative. Previously only made of cardboard, file boxes are now available in strong waterproof plastic or rubber containers. They come in bright colours or are transparent. Their ability to be stacked one atop the other enables you to move them easily. If you have a project filed in one box, you can carry that box to another room or even to the car. The research materials and drafts for the books I write are kept in separate plastic file boxes. If I need a change of scenery from my study, I can tote my laptop and a file box to another room or into the car for a weekend getaway writing retreat.

Filing

The 'piling' system is okay if you can still quickly find what you're looking for but most people fail in their piling because piles grow. If it takes more than 30 seconds to find something, then the piling system isn't working. For most people, piles of paper, magazines and books impede the search. The same items get handled again and again, being moved from here to there while looking for something else. Piles are usually stacks of 'I-don't-know-what-to-do-with-this' items. Piling can be resolved by creating files as well as throwing much of the incoming paper directly into the rubbish.

If you'd rather pile than file, ask yourself the following:

- Do I always find what I need within 30 seconds?
- Am I happy and relaxed while working in this environment?
- Do I get the job done on time without panicking in paper?
- Would there be benefits if I were better organized anyway?

Let's assume you've now bought yourself some attractive hanging files, colourful file tabs and a filing cabinet or boxes. How will you use them? Here are some tips for practical filing:

Label your files with file tabs, and file them systematically, such as alphabetically.

Keep a file for similar articles. If you are asked to give a talk on Ḥuqúqu'lláh and have kept clippings in a 'Ḥuqúqu'lláh' file over the last year, when you sit down to prepare your talk, half of your work is already done.

Keep all of your owner's manuals and warranties from

items you have purchased in one file. Forgotten how to duplicate videos on your VCR? The instructions are in your file.

The following are common file headings. Create more of your own!

- Bills to pay
- Receipts from purchases – temporary (in case of returns)
- Receipts from purchases – save
- Income tax data
- Health records
- Kids' school records
- Articles to read soon or throw out
- Articles to keep
- Manuals and warranties
- Fireside guests
- Bahá'í lectures and quotations
- Personal letters
- Photographs
- Minutes from LSA or committee meetings
- Ongoing project for LSA or committee
- Insurance
- Investments
- Bank and credit card statements
- Maps

Make a file called 'Directions'. In it you keep the addresses and directions to obscure locations and friends' homes you don't go to regularly. People usually write directions on a scrap of paper and discard it after their arrival, needing to call for directions to the same place next time. If you have a file for 'Directions' you will always know how to get where you're going.

Consider having personal calling cards printed with your home address, phone number, fax and email. If your home is hard to find, have a map or directions printed on the reverse side! Your friends will appreciate your orderliness and consideration. You could also have a map and directions to your home on a computer file, to easily email them to guests.

A retired gentleman who has now made being organized his favourite hobby gave a very thoughtful gift to each of his four adult children last Ayyám-i-Há. He bought each of them an attractive two-drawer filing cabinet. He filled the cabinets with empty files and labelled each one with headings he thought his children would use. It was a practical and much appreciated gift! One of his daughters told me she always wanted to be the kind of person who filed things but she never got around to it. The nudge her father gave her was all she needed to get organized.

Taking Notes

Making note of interesting facts and comments is common practice for Bahá'ís. Whether it's while attending a talk given by a visiting Counsellor or National Spiritual Assembly member or during consultation with friends, Bahá'ís have their minds enriched in numerous ways. A talk given by a prominent person is an occasion one can anticipate hearing something of interest and worth remembering. You can be quite certain the invited speaker will say at least one thing to which your mental response will be, 'Hey, that's a good point! I want to remember that!' And you will forget that brilliant insight before the drive home. Or you will half remember it but butcher it so badly that you cannot use the quotation yourself with any certainty of fact.

Experienced Bahá'ís (meaning the ones who have forgotten quotations several times in the past!) are the ones who now show up at talks and deepenings with note pads. The organized Bahá'ís are the ones who have designated notebooks which travel with them to all lectures. Months later, if they want to retrieve an anecdote or statistic, they know exactly where to find it: in the book where all their notes are. Rereading your notebooks from years past can be quite a shocking experience. The highlights are presented to you again and inspire you once more. It is also a humbling reminder of just how much a person really does forget. Despite thinking 'I'll never forget that!' at the time, we do.

A tip for good note-taking: At the top of each page write the date, speaker and location of each talk, for ease of reference. A ring binder allows you the option of removing and filing pages.

Processing, aka Through-put

Filing implies you are finished with something and just need to put it away. The reason so many people have a clutter problem is because they need to develop a *processing* system. Processing refers to how you handle daily mail and works in progress that are prone to camouflage your desk, night stand, kitchen counter and any other bare surface areas in your home. Visual clutter adds to mental clutter. It is distracting, even stressful. By organizing your living space you work more effectively and reduce stress.

Have a file or desktop basket for items that will expire, such as discount coupons, notices, contest entry forms and so on. If you see an advertisement in the newspaper for a concert or lecture that mildly interests you, clip out the ad and put it in this file or basket. If you decide to go, the information is in the basket. Chances are, though, you will forget about the event. Instead of having saved the whole newspaper in a pile, the ad is in your 'will expire' basket. At least once a month go through this basket and discard all the expired items in it.

Put torn out magazine articles and flyers in this basket. It is much easier than trying to remember why you saved the whole magazine. If you haven't read the article or bought the on-sale item by a certain date, throw the article or flyer out. Don't feel guilty about not reading or responding to these items. Take pleasure in lightening your load.

Create a file called 'month end' or 'Mondays' or what ever time of the week or month you choose to do your business like paying bills and responding to other mail. All your 'to do' items are ready in there without you searching the house to find where you left them. In this file you can put notes to yourself for items on which you have given yourself a deadline to make a decision. Decided to attend a convention that intrigues you? The enrolment form is in this file, right where you put it.

Some people have a file for each day of the week, where their notes to self, bills, etc. are placed. Once a day they spend a few minutes doing the few items they placed in that file. They find this better than having Post-it® Notes haunting them everywhere.

Once you have organized your home office, be aware if your new system starts to slide. Catch yourself as you are about to revert to the piling system. You'll tell yourself, 'I'll just pile these things here for now and sort them tomorrow.' That's the kind of thinking that got you disorganized in the first place! Put your new habits into overdrive! Deal with that piece of paper *now*. Tidying as you go is the easiest way to prevent chaos in your office, kitchen or any room.

Throw It Out!

Shelf junk and desk clutter are cancerous. They spread and take over territory, making it difficult for you to work. How much more efficient you are when you can find what you want! The tidier your work area is, the more focused and productive you are. Many of the paper items in your home office would be better off meeting their destiny in the waste basket.

I do sympathize with how difficult letting go can be, even when the items in question are merely pieces of paper. Yet I must still adamantly state, 'If in doubt, throw it out!' If you have to ask yourself the question, 'Should I keep this?' the fact that it is not an obvious keeper is your cue to throw it out. You can streamline stored information with computer and paper files. Most of the rest can go. Much of the information cluttering your shelves, like old magazines, is unnecessary.

The same is true for papers people store in boxes, like old school books and essays. If you haven't reread

Beware if your new system starts to slide

them since school, you surely aren't going to now. Cut the cord and let them go.

If a magazine article is especially interesting and you really will use it again, tear out the article and keep it in a file. One page stored in a file takes up a lot less space than storing the whole magazine on a shelf or in a box.

I once read a newspaper article about a woman who poured gasoline on herself and set herself afire on a university campus in a desperate attempt to draw attention to the issue of world peace. She was an activist who felt the world wasn't listening. She gave her life to draw attention to the cause she believed in. Possibly the woman was mentally ill but that doesn't matter. She died tragically because she felt alone in her pleas for world unity.

I wondered if the woman might not have taken such drastic measures had she met a Bahá'í in her city and been introduced to the teachings of Bahá'u'lláh. I believe she would have liked to know that a blueprint for a divine new world order is at hand and that she would be welcomed by the Bahá'ís in our Cause! I also wondered how many other people are out there feeling helpless and depressed. That article reminded me how important it is to teach, teach, teach. Tell everyone about Bahá'u'lláh!

I clipped that article out of the newspaper, unsure when I would use it. But I couldn't throw it away. Someone died because she saw no hope for peace and unity in our world. It went in my 'articles for talks' file. Perhaps I'll use her story one day in a talk on the urgency to teach.

Mail

In North America we now receive as much mail in a day as our parents did in a week. I have a friend with a sign on her mailbox: 'No junk mail please! Family under paper stress!'

With the advent of the Internet, much regular mail has been reduced but 'snail mail' does still exist and will continue to do so. There are ways to reduce one's paper overload and deal with incoming mail effectively.

Just because something arrives in your mailbox doesn't mean you have to open it. Throw out unsolicited mail without even reading it. Just because the pizza flyer and contest entry were addressed to you doesn't mean you have to read them. I belong to an association that puts out a quarterly magazine that seldom has an article of interest to me. Despite my repeated requests that they not send me the magazine, it keeps coming. They have not yet devised a method for keeping my name *on* their membership list but *off* their bulk mail list. Guilt-free, I toss the publication into my recycling basket the moment it arrives without even opening the cover.

Time management experts say, 'Handle a piece of paper only once.' Pay a bill when you open it. Respond to a request right away. Sometimes you can't deal with paper mail immediately, though. You want to check with your spouse's schedule before accepting a wedding invitation. You can't renew the insurance policy until next pay day. If you cannot act upon a piece of mail immediately, at least move it forward a little. Do not set it back in your mail pile. Move these items to their appropriate 'to do by such a date' folders so that you are not wasting time handling the same envelope several times without dealing with the matter. Don't linger while opening mail. Make decisions: rubbish, respond or file it.

Always have a stock of various envelopes and stamps on hand. Not having the right sized envelope or number of stamps is frequently the reason people don't do their snail mail in a timely fashion. Having the right tools for the job enables you to finish with a piece of mail when you first open it.

Decreasing Mail

There are ways you can minimize the amount of snail mail you receive:

Wherever possible, arrange for automatic payment of bills through your bank.

Think twice before giving your name and address to a business. You might be added to another mailing list or have your name and address sold to services that want new names for their lists. Most businesses, such as clothing stores, do not need your home address and phone number for you to make a purchase, so don't give it out if they ask at the till.

Think twice before entering your name in a 'free' draw. Giving away prizes is a popular method used to gather new names for mailing lists.

When you give your name and address to a group – for example, when making a contribution to a worthy charity – ask if they sell their mailing list. Groups who need to raise funds will do what they can to increase their revenue, including selling their mailing lists. You can specify that you want to contribute to their cause but that your name cannot be sold with their list. To keep you as a contributor, they will oblige.

One year I was inundated with requests for donations from new charities on an unprecedented scale. Owing to the same peculiar misspelling of my name, I surmised they all acquired my name from the same source. By phoning the head office of each group I learned how forthcoming they were about where they purchased my name. (A numeric code in my address label revealed all.) Each organization graciously removed my name from its list and the environmental group that precipitated all this unsolicited mail learned that while I appreciated the work they were doing, they were never again to sell my name to anybody. They have obliged.

To further facilitate having their names removed from mailing lists Canadians can write to the Canadian Marketing Assn, Do Not Mail/Do Not Call Service, Box 706 Don Mills, Ontario, M3C 2T6, or call (416) 391–2362.

For residents of the USA, contact the Direct Marketing Association, 1120 Avenue of the Americas, New York, New York, 10036–6700, or call (212) 768–7277.

Your country likely has an equivalent service too!

Do you keep getting junk mail from a particular company? On the unopened envelope write 'Moved. Return to sender' and drop it back into the mailbox. When this doesn't work, I write 'DECEASED. Return to sender.' To stop unsolicited mail I have effectively feigned my own death a few times. It works!

Working from Home

Working from home used to mean a person was not a true professional or wasn't successful enough to afford a real office. With the advances in telecommunications, working from home is not only now respected, it is envied. To walk down your own hall and be in your office in five seconds is an appealing alternative for people who routinely have to negotiate rush hour traffic. Many employers find it cost-effective to provide employees with fax machines, computers and modems to be used in their own homes. As long as the work is submitted on time and accurately, it matters not if the employee doing the job is in the same building as management or in another country.

Although the lifestyle of working from home sounds attractive, it is not for everyone. The temptations of home are all around you. A trip to the fridge when you hit a creative block is too easy, especially if no one else is home.

Keeping It Professional

Adhering to the following rules helps those who work at home maintain their professionalism:

Create a professional-looking work space for yourself. This is your job, so take it seriously.

Set specific work hours and keep to them. Get up, get

showered and dressed as if you were leaving for the office. Wearing a tie is not necessary but a clean shirt and trousers are. Slippers are acceptable home office attire.

If your children are young and need supervision, another adult or teen should be in the house for childcare. Don't kid yourself that you can be a professional working in your home office and perform childcare at the same time.

Tell your family members what your working hours are. A sign on your closed office door saying 'Mummy's Working' will help them respect your work times. Let them know when you are next available. Hang a cardboard clock on the door with the hands showing at what time you will next surface from your den. Practising the virtue of patience, your children can hold their requests until then. They can also answer the family phone and take written messages.

Give your friends your work hours and ask them not to call at these times. Someone working at home is perceived always to be available to others. 'Jane's home during the day. I'll ask *her* when the next Feast is.' If your friends wouldn't interrupt you at your office outside of the home, they shouldn't call you at your home office with the same questions either. If your personal phone rings, let the machine take a message. A friend told me, 'When I first started working from home, my neighbours used to drop in on me as they had done before I started work. I used to drive my car around the corner so people thought I was away. It worked!'

Consider getting a separate business telephone line or cell phone. If this line rings, you know it's business and you can answer.

Watch out for interruptions from yourself. If you wouldn't make frequent trips to the fridge while out in the work force, don't do it during home office hours either!

8
Technology

I do not fear computers. I fear the lack of them.
Isaac Asimov

Love 'em or hate 'em, computers are here to stay. They are an inevitable step in an ever-advancing global society. People can now work from home, email friends around the world, shop on the Internet and more. Whether you feel computers have put more or less time into your hands is another story.

Techno-stress

The Internet, laptops, cell phones, Palm Pilots® and other techno-tools have made our lives easier in many ways and provided us with new sources of entertainment. They have also contributed to a new form of anxiety called 'techno-stress'.

Information now bombards us at dizzying speed. Many western homes have 50 or more television channels, all providing us with endless information. (I grew up with two black and white channels and don't recall complaining that 'there's nothing on TV'.) This barrage leaves many people feeling they are unable to keep up with the world. Information floods in faster than a person can learn or retain it. Many people feel stressed owing to their own belief that they must keep up. Keep

up with what? The availability of information? Nowadays that is a totally unrealistic expectation. It is humanly impossible to keep up with all that is new, even within one's own profession, in many cases.

Our great-grandparents received mail at best once a week, news was often old by the time it was in print and there was no television or email providing instant information. Our ancestors were more focused on meeting each day's needs than we are. They may have had more physical challenges in coping each day but they were not stressed trying to keep up with the information age. I bet they slept better than we do too.

To break free from techno-stress, decide how much

info-input is reasonable for you. How much is a reasonable amount of time a week to devote to learning what's new in your profession? Do you read the morning paper because you feel you have to or is it genuinely a relaxing time for you? Do you hoard magazines, newspapers, articles or books because they contain information you think you must keep? Do you receive, and respond to, more emails than you ever thought you would?

Also accept that you do not have to store information (in files, in boxes or in your head) in case you need it someday. We now live in a time when having the skills to find information is of greater value than actually storing hard copies of data.

How Much Computer Do You Need?

Given the speed at which technology is advancing, it would not be wise for me to recommend particular computer hardware and software to busy Bahá'ís. Before this book is off the press the information will be obsolete. There are some suggestions, though, that endure the test of time.

When shopping for computer hardware or software, 'buy only what you need and the best that you can afford'. If you know that for the next couple of years you only intend to write personal emails, keep committee minutes and learn to surf the net, don't waste your money also buying a colour laser printer. By the time you do have the need for sophisticated printing, a better printer at a lower price could be on the market. Buy as much computer memory as your budget permits for you to work efficiently. Accept that technology is always changing and once you buy something it will no longer be the latest model. Next month someone will have produced a newer, smaller, faster electronic toy. You don't have to have the very best; you only need to have what you need. Don't spend money unnecessarily on features you won't use.

Spend the time required to learn to use your equipment. Read the owner's manual. (Most people never do until they are in a crisis.) Take a class. Some stores offer introductory lessons if you purchase products from them. From a time management perspective, learning to use your equipment when you first bring it home is critical. Your fax machine will wait to jam until you are in a hurry and can't afford a delay. Your files will fail to attach to emails only on the day the information is vital to the receiver. Learn how to problem-solve before you have an emergency.

Save your material as you write it. Back it up on disk. Print hard copies of really valuable material. (My manuscripts, for example, are printed even when they still look sloppy. The thought of losing years of typing and creative thinking is unbearable). Saving files is common sense, but people procrastinate. Most computer users have at least one horror story of a costly crash or accidental deletion of an important file.

Email

Email Phobia

A few people among us are still phobic when it comes to email. While one does not have to learn all the clever functions hidden within computers, being able to communicate by email is now a reasonable expectation in our society. Email is now as essential as the telephone. If you don't have it, you are excluding yourself from the flow of communication.

When the telephone was first invented there were people who didn't get phones because their lives functioned very well without them. Some even thought the telephone was evil and technology had gone too far. If you don't have email at home because you can't afford a computer, that's understandable. But if you're trying to prove your independence from technology, think again. The telephone is now a standard feature in modern homes and email is following closely.

Once people get online they wonder how they functioned without email and don't want to give it up. If you are the only Assembly or committee member not on email, consider how you might be impeding the communication of the whole group. If you think you don't need email, then get rid of your telephone, too, and see how it feels! Not to be able to communicate with others (by phone or email) could affect your service as a Bahá'í. Do not be afraid. Email *is* easily learned. Ask a trusted friend to help you get started and soon you will be amazed at the wonders of 'being connected'!

Email is there for *you* to use; don't let *it* use *you*. Be stingy with your address unless you want unsolicited email. If a friend puts you on his 'joke list' without asking you first and you're getting excessive unsolicited mail, ask him to remove your name. To be on several email lists can result in a high volume of daily mail, all of which requires time to read. Be sure that's how you enjoy spending your time and you're not reading 'list email' just because people send you trivia.

Email Etiquette

When email came on the scene there was no precedent for the 'right' way to write email notes. Is it okay to be really brief? Do I still say 'Dear Joanne' as I would in a paper letter? In the short time that email has been around, some general principles of etiquette have emerged.

Yes, it's okay to be very brief. One politely written sentence asking a specific question or responding with only the answer to a question asked is acceptable email etiquette.

It is appropriate to address the person, such as starting with 'Dear Bob' or 'Hi Maggie'. Email is frequently less formal than paper communication for personal correspondence.

Don't say anything on email you wouldn't say out loud. A poor choice of words can be saved by the recipient or forwarded to other people.

Keep emails brief if you want them to be read. Many people have personal policies of deleting long emails the moment they become tiresome, without finishing reading them.

Keep to only one subject per email. If you have two questions to ask your fellow Assembly members, one to establish if there is a quorum for the next meeting and the other to ask if a van is still needed for the youth travel teaching trip, don't put them in the same email!

Title one 'Quorum' and the other 'Van'. People will respond to the items separately, when they know the answers to each of your questions.

Use the subject line for the actual subject. If the above two emails were combined and the subject line read 'Hi from Frank', the reader doesn't know the topic of the email. Busy people have to select which emails get read first and a clear subject line helps. 'Hi from Frank' looks unimportant and chatty and might not be opened until later. 'LSA Quorum', however, is understandably urgent. A clear subject line is also a courtesy to the recipient. Saved emails are easier to file and find again when the subject lines are clear.

Reply on topic, otherwise change the subject line. If someone sends you an email entitled 'teaching project' and you want to write back to that person asking where the next Feast is, change the subject line if you're using your reply feature. Otherwise, write a new email.

Some attempts at humour, such as sarcasm or understatements, do not necessarily email well. They can be taken literally by the reader. Use indirect humour only if the reader knows you well and can 'hear' your voice while reading.

Writing in upper case letters is considered SHOUTING, email style. Don't use it unless you would raise your voice in person.

Have a recognizable email address, preferably with your name in it. This is a courtesy to the recipients of your emails. If you must have an alias for other purposes, have a separate 'named' account for your friends and your Bahá'í correspondence.

Email Ease

The advent of email has brought a new kind of stress but some principles, when followed, will protect you from email stress.

Delete as you go. Learn to recognize what is 'trash' worthy after being read once and put it there immediately.

Create files! Don't leave everything in your 'in' file. Open *lots* of files, such as Assembly minutes, teaching stories, committee mandates, jokes, letters from family and so on. Group similar items together and file them. As with paper files, create a 'will expire' file. Once a month delete all messages a month old without rereading them. The expiry date has passed and you don't need to relive the advertisement.

Create name lists. A grouping called 'Teaching Committee' can contain all six members' email addresses, saving you having to type all six names each time you write to them.

Get virus protection for your computer. Some malicious people create and send computer viruses to hundreds of thousands of people through unsolicited email.

Telephones

Gone are the days of getting on your horse and riding three miles to give a message to your neighbour. The telephone is a definite time-saver. For many people it is a social and recreational tool as well. Just ask any teenager! We can shop by phone. Work by phone. The elderly or infirm feel more secure knowing help is just a call away.

But having a telephone also makes a person more accessible. At times your privacy can feel invaded. Cell phones are convenient, even fun, but just how accessible do you want to be? Do you want to be frequently interrupted? Some people need their cell phones for business. Parents are reassured knowing that their children can reach them whenever they need to. Beyond these kinds of uses, caution should be exercised over how many people you give your cell number to. If you are feeling stressed from the busy-ness of your life, make sure your cell phone is actually being used for *your* comfort and convenience and not as another way the world can close in on you.

How much time do you spend on the phone? If you have a hunch that you talk too long on the phone, you probably do. As an experiment, keep a phone log for a few days. Write down how many minutes each call takes and note the total each day. You might be shocked by how much time you unnecessarily spend on the telephone.

If you are someone who is good at keeping your calls short, you might feel trapped by others who love to chat endlessly. I have one girlfriend with whom each call will be 15 minutes, minimum. She'll be hurt if I just deal with the purpose of the call and don't visit for longer. There are some techniques for streamlining phone calls:

With the above mentioned girlfriend, I use the speaker phone. I file my nails or do light housekeeping while listening to her.

At the outset of an in-coming call, state how much time you have. 'Yes, I'm free to talk. I have five minutes until I have to go out.'

For out-going calls state what needs to be achieved. 'Bob, do you have a couple minutes to consult? I hear you can recommend a good DJ for the Naw-Rúz party.'

Purposely call and leave a message that does not need to be returned when you know someone isn't in. That's the shortest 'conversation' of all! 'Karen, I have the book you are looking for and I'll bring it to Feast tomorrow night.'

When you get an answering machine, give complete messages to reduce telephone tag. Instead of saying, 'Hi Ben. Please call me back,' say, 'The other members of our task force are able to meet Friday, 8:00 p.m. at Raj's house. Is this time good for you?'

Just because the telephone is ringing, you are not obliged to jump to answer it right away! Listen to Evelyn's story:

> My son and I were discussing what he was going to do one evening. A new acquaintance of his was pressuring him to go out that evening and my son didn't really like associating with this boy. My son is easily swayed by others and I could see he might easily give in to the other boy's wishes tonight. During our discussion the phone rang. On the phone display we could see the in-coming call was from the boy we were talking about. My son reached for the phone.
> 'Wait!' I said. 'What are you going to tell him?'
> 'I don't know.'
> 'Can we finish our discussion first then?'
> 'But the phone's ringing!'
> 'So let it ring! You can call him back.'
> We talked for another five minutes until my son got his thoughts clear. He called the boy and said he wanted to stay home this evening. I was so proud of him for standing up for himself!

It takes practice not to answer the phone. With Pavlovian speed, we react to the sound of the bell. Practise pausing before answering and ask yourself if you really should take a call right now. As a courtesy to others, answer whenever possible. But if the timing is really bad for you, let the answering service take a message.

Comedian Jerry Seinfeld jokes about annoying telephone sales people who call you at home during supper hour. Seinfeld's solution: Ask the sales person for *his* home phone number and tell him you will call back when *he* is having supper!

Samir's story:

When our answering machine broke my wife and I procrastinated about replacing it. We were both too busy to go shopping. For one month we had no answering machine. It was such a relief to come home after work and not have half a dozen calls to return! We eventually subscribed to an answering service because we both are active Bahá'ís and agreed we can serve the Faith better if friends can reach us. I know the frustration of trying to reach someone who doesn't have an answering service. But that one month reprieve taught us a lesson. We learned how much stress the telephone causes in our lives. From then on we have made it a habit to enjoy supper together before listening to our messages.

Other ways to reduce telephone stress:

Turn the ringer volume down. The less jarring the noise, the more calm you will be while approaching the phone.

Turn the phone off during meals, love-making or other times when an interruption would really not be appreciated.

Give yourself a night off from the phone once in a while. If any messages come in, check them the next morning.

Kids and the Phone

Teach your children that use of the telephone is a privilege. They may answer the phone if they use the script you teach them, such as 'Smith residence. Jason speaking.'

Never should your children tell a caller they are home alone. If kids are of an age where they can be left for short periods, they should take a message for you, saying you are unable to come to the phone at the moment.

Have a pen and paper beside the phone for your kids to take your messages. You can write 'name: _____, number: _____' on a few pages to cue your child what to ask the caller. Kids often get the content of a message skewed. Be satisfied if they can get a caller's name and number.

Buy a toy telephone for a toddler who thinks your phone is his toy.

Consider having a separate line and phone number for your teenagers. It may cost a little extra but the elimination of fights over the phone is worth it. You can arrange that the kids' line is barred from making long distance calls.

More Phone Tips

Before placing a call, gather the resources you need, such as a pen and note pad, phone numbers and relevant documents for the purpose of the call.

Purchase a headset if you make a lot of phone calls. They are available for home use and are not only for professional receptionists.

If you don't have your notebook with you and need to write something down when you're not at home, phone yourself! Phone home and talk to your own answering machine/voice mail. You can transcribe the information later once you're home.

The conference call does wonders for saving commuting time. Small committees are better able to keep up with their agendas if they have brief conference calls between their regular meetings. If you haven't tried conference calling yet, give it a go!

9

Time Management for Your Health

> Every man dies,
> but not every man lives.

Managing our time well isn't something that would be nice to do if only we could get our act together some day. Good time management is a critical necessity for our health. Our mental, physical, spiritual and emotional well-being is dependent on how responsibly we manage our lives.

How would you assess your current success at managing your life? Would you say you are coping? sinking? living fully?

Coping means you are just getting things done. Most tasks are completed on time but often you feel rushed. And you hope no one sees how messy your bedroom really is.

Sinking is self-explanatory. 'The faster I go, the behinder I get,' some people say.

People who are living fully stand up on their surfboards and ride the waves with style. There is an expression 'Your life is not a dress rehearsal'. This is the real thing. Maximize your life by treating your time as valuable as gold.

Being Here Now

> Give us our daily bread, and grant Thine increase in the necessities of life, that we may be dependent on none other but Thee, may commune wholly with Thee, may walk in Thy ways and declare Thy mysteries. Thou art the Almighty and the Loving and the Provider of all mankind.
> *'Abdu'l-Bahá'*

In the Bible the Lord's Prayer says, 'Give us this day our daily bread.' Note that neither this prayer nor 'Abdu'l-Bahá's says, 'Give us our annual bread and guarantee us a comfortable and early retirement.' While it is appropriate to be aware of our future and it is wise to plan well for it, we must not overlook the blessings of our present moments. Prayer is a prime example of 'being in the now'.

> Being in the here and now is a gift.
> That's why they call it 'the present'.

If you are under stress and need practice being here now, spend some time playing with a dog or a baby. They will teach you quickly. The dog doesn't worry that he may have offended someone last night or how the stock market changes will affect the price of dog food. He just wants to enjoy your company as you scratch behind his ears. A baby on your lap has no past or future cares either. The two of you sit staring into each other's eyes, while your voice goes up an octave as you babble in baby talk. Dogs and babies are perfect here and now ambassadors, no doubt sent here with mandates to rescue the rest of us into timeless moments as often as possible.

If you are under stress and need practice
being here now, spend some time playing with a
dog or a baby.

The trouble with you is you never live in the here and now.
You live in the there and then.
I, however, live in the here and there now and then!
Dudley Moore

Solitude

I would rather sit on a pumpkin
and have it all to myself,
than be crowded on a velvet cushion.
Thoreau

When I first read that quotation from Thoreau my immediate response was a yearning to throw my arms around him and say, 'Yes! Yes! I know exactly what you mean!' But in doing so I would be crowding him on a velvet cushion, so I must instead admire his prose from the solitude of my own pumpkin.

People have varying needs for solitude. Mine is great. I need at least four hours alone every day. I write, meditate, pray, exercise or just lie about but I need to do it alone. That can be very hard to protect sometimes. When I am on a writing spree I can go into solitude for 48 hours straight. I type, eat and sleep. I don't even notice the absence of others. A writer's life could make normal people go bonkers.

I have sympathy for people who do not get enough solitude. Members of a large family living in tight quarters, for example, or a mother who is always 'on duty' might crave more solitude. My sister was taking a correspondence course in interior design when she had her first baby. Being on maternity leave from her full-time job, she anticipated getting ahead in her design course.

One day I called and asked, among other things, how her schooling was coming along. 'School?' she said. 'I don't even have time to take a bath!' She was 'blessed' with a baby who thought naps were only for old people.

While our needs for solitude vary, all Bahá'ís have the same daily minimum requirement: we pray, in private, one to three times a day, depending on the obligatory prayer we select. In that moment nothing else matters. There is you and your spiritual union with Bahá'u'lláh. Once you have sequestered yourself in a private section of your busy home, you are there in a state of prayer. Maximize this time. Before or after your obligatory prayer, meditate. The merry-go-round of your life can wait until after your sacred time of prayer.

Meditation

> For him who has no concentration,
> there is no tranquillity.
> *Bhagavad Gita*

One of the many things that attracted me to the Bahá'í Faith was prayer. I liked to pray but had few friends I could admit that to and fewer yet with whom I could pray. I did enjoy meditating alone and with friends. Then I met the Bahá'ís. Great people, dripping with integrity, and they prayed together. These were friends I wanted to be with!

It was not long before I noticed that prayer over-shadowed meditation. Bahá'ís talked about 'prayer and meditation' as if they were both important but I only saw them pray together. So I asked people if they meditated at home alone. 'Yeah, sometimes. But I'd like to do it more,' was the usual response. Over a decade later and I'm still asking Bahá'ís about their meditation practices. The responses haven't changed. Bahá'ís acknowledge the importance of meditation, yet few I've met prioritize it and meditate daily.

Once you develop the habit of daily meditation, you cannot live well without it. If you omit it one day, something feels awkwardly wrong. It's like leaving the house in the morning without having brushed your teeth. You feel uncomfortable, knowing you forgot something important. To reach the point where you feel out of sorts if you don't meditate is a good thing! It means regular meditation has been putting something qualitatively grand into your life.

If you find yourself avoiding meditating, ask yourself 'What else do I need to do today that is more important?' In this perspective, your other 'obligations' can look rather silly.

> Through the faculty of meditation man attains to eternal life;
> through it he receives the breath of the Holy Spirit –
> the bestowal of the Spirit is given in reflection and meditation.

> The spirit of man is itself informed and strengthened during meditation;
> through it affairs of which man knew nothing are unfolded before his view.
> Through it he receives Divine inspiration,
> through it he receives heavenly food.

Meditation is the key for opening the doors of mysteries.
In that state man abstracts himself:
in that state man withdraws himself from all outside objects;
in that subjective mood he is immersed in the ocean of
spiritual life
and can unfold the secrets of things-in-themselves.
'Abdu'l-Bahá

If you are wondering what meditation is, or how to do it, it does not have to be complicated. You do not need to take a course to learn it, though some courses are offered and many meditation books and CDs are on the market.

Meditation can be as simple as sitting in a comfortable position (no tricky pose required) and closing your eyes for five minutes. Just focus on breathing slowly and deeply. If unwanted thoughts come into your head, like things you need to do later, don't follow these thoughts with self-criticism for being a 'poor meditator'. Let the thoughts move on and you go back to focusing on breathing. A few minutes of this is meditating.

You do not have to stay there for an hour for it to be done 'right'. As you practise daily, your ability to tune out distractions will improve and you might choose to meditate for longer periods. The benefits derived from meditation include feeling calm, clearer thinking and increased energy. That's quite a good return on a few minutes' investment!

Silence

True silence is the rest of the mind;
it is to the spirit what sleep is to the body,
nourishment and refreshment.
William Penn

One benefit of solitude and meditation is silence. When you are alone, there is an increased probability that you will be quiet.

If you would like to increase the amount of serenity in your life instantly, do the following experiment: *Be quiet more often in the company of others.* It is a marvellous barometer of how much we say that is not necessary! Other people feel you are such a good listener, your negative thoughts are not given voice and generally there is an air of calm around you. Both you and the people around you will feel it. 'My, isn't she serene,' they will think. 'My, doesn't it feel great not to talk unnecessarily,' you will think.

Recall the opening line from the wise piece of prose entitled 'Desiderata':

> Go placidly amid the noise and haste
> and remember what peace there may be in silence.

Those are words worth living by!

Daydreaming

> Cherish your visions and your dreams
> as they are the children of your soul,
> the blueprints of your ultimate achievements.
> *Napoleon Hill*

Daydreams are wonderful! Daydreams are mental mini-vacations that happen numerous times a day. You can't stop them. You'll be working on a task and suddenly find yourself staring off, thinking about something totally unrelated. Unless you do more daydreaming than working, don't worry about it. You can't cycle up-hill all day. You need to coast and glide periodically.

It is in those daydreaming moments that creativity flourishes. Inventions are born, problems are solved. Some of history's greatest minds did their best work while daydreaming. Albert Einstein said, 'When I examine myself and my methods of thought, I come to the conclusion that the gift of fantasy has meant more to me than my talent for absorbing positive knowledge.'

There is merit in doing 'nothing' for a brief time. It is physically resting. It is a mental break from your tasks. It also helps you realize how slow time really is. If you think you 'don't have time', just sit and watch time for five minutes. Do nothing with your hands, no reading or watching TV, no meditating. Just sit and watch time. It goes so slowly. Five minutes is often more than a person can tolerate before getting restless and wanting to get involved again.

Diet and Exercise

There are nine topics covered in the Health chapter of this book and it might surprise you that only one of them refers to diet and exercise. The aforementioned subjects such as meditation and solitude are health necessities too. While there is much I would like to say on the matters of diet and exercise, many fine authors have already written volumes on these two subjects, so I can limit my rants to a few selected highlights.

Obesity is dangerously on the rise, with 55 per cent of Americans being overweight. One-sixth are obese. The fastest rate of increasing obesity is in American children, a quarter of whom are already overweight.

Obesity has been declared a national epidemic!

This is not a book on nutrition, so I won't expound on it here. But nutrition is a vitally important subject. If you are not practising good nutrition and you are not a healthy weight, please get some help. Read books. Join Weight Watchers. See your doctor. Do whatever you need to do to feed your body respectfully.

In 'Abdu'l-Bahá's own words, 'The golden rule as to food is, do not take too much or too little. Moderation is necessary.'[3]

We All Need Exercise

If at the age of 50 you weigh the same as you did when you were 20, you might be wondering why you don't look the same as you did in your youth. Unless you have been exercising regularly, your muscle/fat ratio has changed owing to decreased activity. Muscle is denser than fat, meaning it weighs more and takes up less space. So even if you weigh the same as you did 30 years ago, chances are you won't fit into the trousers you wore back then. Exercise is not just a young

person's game. In fact, the older we get the more delib-
erate we have to be to keep our parts in working order.

Think you don't have time for cardiovascular exercise? Hidden exercise opportunities are all around you,
such as taking the stairs for a few flights instead of the
elevator. Walk to the convenience store rather than
drive. Do jumping jacks while watching TV. If you put
'20 minutes cardio workout' on your 'To Do' list, you
will give it time.

Strength Training

Most people understand the merits of getting regular
cardiovascular exercise but the word is only slowly
getting around regarding the important role strength
training (weightlifting) plays for *everyone*. Strength
training is a necessary adjunct to any cardiovascular
exercise programme.

I have a girlfriend who prided herself on being ultra
skinny. 'Why would I want to lift weights?' she scoffed.
'I don't want big muscles!'

'So that one day when you're older and fall on your
hip, you bounce right back up again without a fracture,'
I told her. She thought that weight training was only for
muscles but now sees its importance for healthy bones
too. She started lifting weights and now looks better than
ever. Her slender frame now has some attractive curves.

Moderate weightlifting will give you a toned body
without bulk. Calcium supplements do their part in
preventing osteoporosis but they alone cannot save your
bones. The way to actually strengthen bones is to *exercise* them. *Strong muscles help make strong bones.* Trust me:
I'm a nurse and long-time weight lifter.

Flexibility

Consider how two 18-year-old boys are relatively alike. Both are strong, fast, and full of energy. Now compare two 70-year-old men. It is possible for one of them to be lean, flexible, strong and planning to live independently for the rest of his life. The other 70-year-old can't tie his shoes any more because his feet are too far away. He already lives in a nursing home. Neither man is suffering from any disease or disorder. When both men were 18 they were relatively alike. Barring any illnesses that would have made the playing field uneven, the different ways in which the two men chose to treat their bodies is what made their outcomes different.

The first man made a point of keeping his parts in working order. He intentionally maintained his flexibility through daily stretching. The man in the nursing home was admitted with the common catch-all diagnosis 'general debility'. It's the 'use it or lose it' syndrome. When we stop putting our bodies through their full range of motion our flexibility and ability to care for ourselves rapidly decline.

Which person do you want to be? The independent and active senior or the one who can no longer dress himself? You *are* going to become one or the other. Fortunately, you really do have a choice, barring a serious medical problem. I have spent my nursing career caring for people of all ages who were in various stages of self-neglect and have too often seen the consequences of laziness and poor self-care.

We lose lean muscle mass weekly, and flexibility daily, when in a state of rest. Fortunately, both can be regained! *If you don't want to lose your physical independence, stretch daily and exercise moderately.* Your future well-being depends on it.

Time for Exercise

The time management implications of having a healthy body are great. Most of us would love to have attractive, slim bodies that don't creak when we bend and we'd like to get these bodies free of charge. Wouldn't it be nice not to have to put any effort into keeping our bodies healthy? If you only use your bicycle in the summer, then dusting it off and oiling it up once a year is okay. But you need your body every day of your life! Not having it in tune spoils your enjoyment of the other things you do. Therefore, this body of yours is going to require daily maintenance, from making responsible food choices (occasional treats are allowed), to stretching and exercising even on days when you really don't feel like it. Spending 20 minutes minimum on self-care each day is not a large demand on your time, especially when you see the benefits. So schedule the best time of your day for yourself and use it for exercise. Your increased energy and vitality will improve your performance in everything else you do too! This is a win-win situation.

The Possession Diet

Want to lose a few pounds? I have a fascinating exercise for you that involves no trips to the gym and no calorie counting: *Purge yourself of your needless possessions.* You read that right. Clean out your storage closet, basement or garage. Thin your clothes closet of items that haven't been worn in the last year. Do the same in your kitchen.

Can't remember when you last used that waffle iron? Get rid of it.

Now what does this have to do with weight loss? Plenty. Your body is a reflection of the condition the rest of your life is in. Excess baggage takes up unnecessary space on your body as well as in your home. Numerous people report having a sudden weight loss after they purge their homes of excess weight.

What is the explanation for this? Somewhere in our psyche there is a link between the 'need' to hoard material goods and the storage of excess body weight. How the mind–body connection works is still being investigated by scientists but with so much anecdotal evidence out there, why not give possession-purging a try? It is such a relief to finally lighten up. Clearing out a burdensome room of your home won't result in a 50-pound weight loss but don't be surprised if you have an effortless drop of five or ten pounds soon after you get your home in order. Really!

Stress

Do you ever feel like a juggler, trying to manage your life? Do you have several balls in the air and every one of them is valuable to you? If you are getting a nudge in your gut that says you are juggling too many balls, then you probably are.

If you are not sleeping adequately, if you are worrying about keeping up with your responsibilities, if your happiness and serenity are slipping away from you, then you *are* too busy. I strongly urge you to set down a ball or two. I don't say this just because it would be nice for you to get caught up. It's far more serious than that.

There is a critical risk when you juggle too much: *You could accidentally drop your most valuable ball.*

If you know that you can reasonably juggle six balls (roles in life), then beware if someone tosses a seventh one at you. It's far better that you voluntarily set down a lower priority ball than drop one that will break your heart.

You might think that if you raise your stress threshold you won't feel the effects of stress so much. Actually the opposite is true. If you raise your stress threshold, you have made more room for stress in your life! People who continually raise their stress thresholds and take on more and more responsibilities are at risk of eventually crashing under the pressure. They get 'stressed out'. Their physical and/or emotional health let go. By keeping your stress threshold at a moderate level, and saying when enough is enough, your life stays manageable.

Doing more tasks faster is not necessarily the best way to cope with stress and feeling behind. The expression 'Sometimes you need to slow down to get ahead' holds true here. Taking the required time to regroup your thoughts or to get adequate rest is precisely what is needed to make progress.

A major cause of stress is the human quest for *sameness*. It is a mistaken interpretation of serenity that assumes peace means everything is calm and no further changes happen. We want to get caught up with our tasks and then have everything stay just as it is. It is the myth of 'As soon as I get (blank) done, then everything will be okay/I will have peace/Then I will be happy'. When we let go of this erroneous belief, an enormous weight is lifted from us. Change is to be accepted as a constant and inevitable force in our lives. True serenity exists when you feel calm despite the fluctuations in the tempo of life around you.

Life can get busy at times. That's accepted. Feeling weighted down with stress, though, is not healthy. How can you tell if you are under too much stress? Ask yourself the following:

> Have I had a recent weight loss or weight gain?
> Do I have trouble going to sleep or staying asleep?
> Do I suffer from constipation or diarrhoea?
> Am I short-tempered or impatient with others?
> Am I more forgetful?
> Do I frequently feel fatigued?
> Do I feel anxious and worried?
> Do I fail to find humour in situations others can laugh at?
> Do I have difficulty making decisions?
> Do I complain frequently?

If you answered 'yes' to three or more of the above questions, you are showing signs of being under too much stress. If the symptoms persist, your health could be in jeopardy. Consult with your physician soon.

If you are feeling 'stressed out' and unable to resolve it, discuss this with your doctor. Many physicians only address a patient's 'presenting complaint' during a visit. Once a year, though, during what is commonly called 'the annual check-up', the physician should be asking more.

Does your physician ask you about your moods, your sleep patterns, the stressors in your life? Good health is far more than normal blood pressure and regular bowel movements. A good physician is not embarrassed to ask about your sex life and whether you are happy in your relationship. If you don't discuss confidential matters with your physician, then how else will you get help? Being stressed, depressed, impotent or sleepless can happen to nice normal people just like you. If you notice you are showing signs of stress and cannot resolve them easily yourself, ask for help. You deserve the confidence of a competent physician with whom you can discuss *anything* – even if it means changing physicians.

Once Upon A Time . . .

there was a very demanding king who revelled in the power his title provided him. No matter what he asked for, his servants brought it. Sometimes the king would invent difficult requests just to see if his servants and advisors could fulfil his whims. They feared the king and the consequences of his displeasure and they always tried their best to please him. One day the king made a request of his advisors that he was certain would stump them.

'I want you to bring me one thing that will make me happy when I am sad and make me sad when I am happy.' The king was delighted with his own creativity. If the advisors did not find a solution for the king they would lose their heads.

The advisors sent the servants searching the countryside looking for one thing that could make the king both happy and sad. The servants returned empty-handed. The advisors consulted for many days, frightened they would lose their heads. Eventually they found an answer for the king. Together they went before him.

'Your Highness, we have found the solution,' they said.

'You have found *one* thing that will make me happy when I am sad and sad when I am happy?' the king asked, sceptically.

'Yes, your Highness, we have.'

'Give it to me, then!' the king demanded.

'When you are happy, your Highness, say to yourself, "This too shall pass". And when you are sad, also say, "This too shall pass".'

The king thought about this for a moment. His advisors kept their heads.

When you find yourself in situations where the stress seems unbearable, remind yourself that 'This too shall pass'.

Unfinished Projects

> Nothing is so fatiguing
> as the eternal hanging on
> of an uncompleted task.
> *William James*

The more tasks you take on, up go the odds that you will have uncompleted work lingering around you. The mental weight of unfinished projects is insidiously great. It gnaws away at your peace of mind.

Make a list of all the started-but-not-finished projects you have at home. Then look at each item and decide to do one of two things: 'Do it or dump it'. (Note that 'Save it for later' is not an option.)

The most effective way to process unfinished tasks is to give yourself permission *not* to do many of them. Have you started a letter but can't seem to get past 'Dear Mary'? Forget the letter. Pick up the phone and give Mary a call, no matter how expensive. As nice as it sounds to say you knit your own sweaters, if a half-knitted sweater has been sitting in your closet for a year, admit that being a sweater-knitter does not rank very high on your 'To Be' list. Throw it out or give the wool to someone who will use it.

Here is one Bahá'í friend's story of simplifying her life by searching through her unfinished projects:

I started sewing a quilt years ago. I was making it from scraps of material from my old clothes over the years. I thought it would be romantic to have a quilt that was like a chronology of my life. I would pick it up from time to time and work on it a little more. But it got to the point where I was doing it out of obligation, doing it just because it was started and not because I enjoyed it. I don't even like the fabrics anymore. I now have other things I'd rather do with my time than sew a quilt. I underestimated how time-consuming it would be.

It was quite an epiphany when I realized I didn't have to finish sewing the quilt! When I mentally gave myself permission to let it go, I felt a weight lifted off me. I was prepared to just throw it out but I found a quilting club that was pleased to have so much material donated and a half-finished quilt, too!

I also took some books to a secondhand bookstore. Some were new hard-cover novels, never read! I bought them on impulse, with intentions of reading them. But I've bought other books since then that I want to read first and I doubted that I'd ever get to those earlier ones. I got some cash for the books. More importantly, they're no longer on my bedside table reminding me of how behind I am with my reading. I've made it a rule: no buying a new book until I'm on the last chapter of the current one. Have I ever saved money on books!

I'm the secretary of our Assembly. Doing the filing is my least favourite job and recently I really let it pile up. I couldn't throw *that* stuff out, so I decided to just do it. It took me 20 minutes! Much less time than I expected. Once it was done I realized that thinking about it and postponing it was a lot worse than actually doing it.

Just Do It.
Nike

Sleep

It should be to such a degree that if he sleep, it should not be for pleasure, but to rest the body in order to do better, to speak better, to explain more beautifully, to serve the servants of God and to prove the truths.   *'Abdu'l-Bahá*[4]

There are three main components commonly accepted as essential for overall health: good nutrition, regular exercise and adequate sleep. Of these three, however, it might surprise you to learn that the element that contributes most to longevity is *sleep*.

A study that compared people who were sporadic with their diet and exercise but slept well nearly every night *outlived* those who were highly disciplined with their diet and exercise programmes but didn't get enough sleep! If you are giving up sleep so you can allegedly 'get more done', with a shortened lifespan you will actually accomplish *less*.

Studies show that sleep-deprived drivers test as poorly as those who are impaired by alcohol. It is estimated that 500,000 automobile accidents happen every year in North America because of drivers falling asleep.

Giraffes sleep two hours a day. Cats sleep for 12. Assuming you are of the human species, your needs fall somewhere in the middle. Prior to Thomas Edison providing us with electric light in 1879, people slept on average ten hours a night. The average North American adult now sleeps seven hours a night. If that's only the average, that means some people are getting much less.

> The sun has not caught me in bed in fifty years.
> *Thomas Jefferson*

Want to know if you are sleeping enough for your individual body's requirements? Here's a simple test*: If you wake up to an alarm clock, you are not sleeping enough.* Your body is designed to wake up naturally when it is finished sleeping. You will not accidentally sleep on and on through eternity if your trusty alarm clock does not wake you up. Your body knows when it wants to stop sleeping all by its clever self. An alarm clock can be kept as a back-up device but most of the time a person should be able to wake up without its aid.

If you get out of bed because your alarm clock has rung, ask yourself the following important question: '*How many other tasks would I settle for doing incompletely?*' Do you set an alarm before you get into the shower and get out when it rings, even if you still have shampoo on your hair? Do you put make-up on the right side of your face but not the left? Do you leave the house with your shirt on and no trousers? If a partially done job with these personal care tasks is not acceptable to you, then why accept sleeping incompletely? You really shouldn't be getting out of bed until your body is finished sleeping! Whether it means going to bed earlier or getting up later, give your body all the sleep that it needs. Your body will show you its gratitude through a healthier immune system and increased energy and alertness.

Take rest; a field that has rested gives a bountiful crop.
Ovid

10

Financial Management

This section on personal finance does not provide comprehensive advice on financial planning. It does, however, look at some key issues where your financial management interlinks with your personal time and life management.

Time Really is Money

Take the following quiz.

Answer with 'always', 'usually', 'seldom' or 'never'. Do you:

> know your monthly income and expenses?
> pay your bills on time?
> file your bills after paying them?
> file your financial documents (bank statements, insurance, etc.)?
> remember to calculate Ḥuqúqu'lláh regularly?
> pay your credit card balance in full each month?
> use automatic payments whenever possible?
> know exactly how and where your money is invested?
> know exactly how much you have in savings and investments?

Answer 'yes' or 'no'. Do you:

- have an ongoing file for documents for your next income tax return?
- have a file (or shoe box or envelope) for receipts of purchases?
- have a regular method for supporting the funds of the Faith?
- have a clear financial plan for retirement?
- have a written legal will?

Management of one's finances is intricately intertwined with how one manages one's time. If you don't have a good grip on the coming and going of your money, I bet you don't know how much time you have either. You likely feel that you don't have enough time OR money.

Not keeping one's financial house in order leads to working more hours to cover debt, spending time worrying or arguing about money, shuffling money from one account to another to cover bills, borrowing and repaying money, and so on. Poor money management does cost time. Eventually, how one manages one's finances determines if and when one retires. Now we're talking about *years* of time linked to financial prudence!

Debt

Credit buying is much like being drunk.
The buzz happens immediately and it gives you a lift.
The hangover comes the day after.
Joyce Brothers

We have become the most heavily indebted generation in history. It has become acceptable to buy a new car with no down payment. Just finance the whole thing. Why save for a new dishwasher or bedroom suite when you can buy now and pay next year, like the TV ads say?

Debt is heavily marketed to you on television and radio. Have you noticed this? Watch more closely the next time you have the TV on. What you think is an advert for a car or new furniture is also an advert for their 'take now and pay later' plan. Then there are the credit card and moneylender adverts. What all these companies are really selling you is debt.

Debt is time-consuming. Shopping to become in debt takes time, arranging financing takes time, juggling accounts to cover debts takes time. So do dodging creditors and returning items to stores.

Worrying over one's debts rapidly promotes the greying of hairs. Spousal arguments over debt are a sad use of a marriage. Money arguments are the leading cause of divorce. Wouldn't you rather do something enjoyable with the person you love than bicker over money?

Not all debt is dumb. Few people can buy a house without a mortgage. Borrowing money to make money is how most businesses get started. But most personal debt troubles exist because people simply lust to live beyond their means. This kind of debt is completely avoidable.

> The bitter taste of debt lasts far longer
> than the sweetness of shopping.

Welcome Wealth

> You can't look after the hard-up people in society
> unless you are accruing enough wealth to do so.
> Good intentions are not enough.
> You do need hard cash.
> *Margaret Thatcher*

Some Bahá'ís are of the belief that to live a spiritual life one must shun affluence. One should spend one's time pursuing spiritual virtues, not money. While chasing the dollar to the exclusion of acquiring virtues would be spiritual suicide, the pursuit of money with virtuous intent is a good thing. Having money is not shameful. What you do with your money, and how detached from it you can be, is what counts.

Should a man wish to adorn himself with the ornaments of the earth, to wear its apparels, or partake of the benefits it can bestow, no harm can befall him, if he alloweth nothing whatever to intervene between him and God, for God hath ordained every good thing, whether created in the heavens or in the earth, for such of His servants as truly believe in Him. Eat ye, O people, of the good things which God hath allowed you, and deprive not yourselves from His wondrous bounties. Render thanks and praise unto Him, and be of them that are truly thankful.

Bahá'u'lláh[1]

Attracting money towards you through sound business and personal decisions gives you more money to circulate. Would you like to be the financial conduit for thousands and thousands of dollars going to worthy charities? Would you like to give copious amounts of cash to your National Spiritual Assembly to help it achieve its goals? Imagine a National Assembly (or other institution of the Faith) only concerning itself with the wise distribution of its endless financial resources rather than worrying about falling short of its budget goals. Let *that* be your vision for your National Spiritual Assembly!

Do not feel guilty if you have attracted great amounts of wealth into your life or if you are planning to. You might inherit money. Perhaps you excel in your profession or are fortunate in business. Whatever your source, spend what you need, then invest and circulate the rest. As the actor Jackie Gleason said, 'The greatest waste of money is to keep it.'

After your own basic needs for food, shelter and the like are met, be generous with the rest. In addition to giving to established charities and Bahá'í funds, sharing smaller sums on a daily basis is extremely rewarding. Give your housekeeper an unexpected bonus; tip the helpful waitress and friendly cab driver extraordinarily. Imagine how appreciated they will feel! You will be spreading wealth and rays of happiness everywhere you go.

Ḥuqúqu'lláh

With increased wealth, despite sharing large amounts of it, most people will spend sums on themselves that go beyond meeting their basic needs. It's one of the perks of success. The houses get bigger, the cars sportier, the clothing and vacations more lavish. Unfortunately, the wealthiest two thousand people in the world have more money than the poorest *two billion combined!* Fortunately, there is a Bahá'í law, Ḥuqúqu-'lláh, that helps to bridge the gap between the extremes of wealth and poverty in our world.

> Should anyone acquire one hundred mithqáls of gold, nineteen mithqáls thereof are God's and to be rendered unto Him, the Fashioner of earth and heaven. Take heed, O people, lest ye deprive yourselves of so great a bounty. This We have commanded you, though We are well able to dispense with you and with all who are in the heavens and on earth; in it there are benefits and wisdoms beyond the ken of anyone but God, the Omniscient, the All-Informed. Say: By this means He hath desired to purify what ye possess and to enable you to draw nigh unto such stations as none can comprehend save those whom God hath willed. He, in truth, is the Beneficent, the Gracious, the Bountiful.   *Bahá'u'lláh*[2]

Nineteen per cent of a Bahá'í's personal profit goes to Ḥuqúqu'lláh, 'the Right of God', which is entrusted to the Centre of the Covenant. Today, this is the Universal House of Justice. The House of Justice distributes this money as it sees fit, for 'All the world hath belonged and will always belong to God'.[3]

The determination of which living expenses are necessary, the calculation of one's personal Ḥuqúqu'lláh and the frequency of the calculation are left to the conscience of the individual believer. Certain possessions are exempt: one's home and its furniture and the tools of one's trade.[4] Beyond this, each person (or couple) is to determine which of his (or their) possessions are needful and which are not.

One person could feel he needs a $20,000 car, another that he needs a $50,000 one. One might consider his car to be a luxury, the other that it is a necessity. It is not only the price of the car that needs to be considered but whether the car itself is necessary. The person who decides that he does not really need a car but would like to have one for pleasure would need to calculate the Ḥuqúqu'lláh due on the price of the car. The person who considers that he needs a car would not pay Ḥuqúq on it.

But consider a third person. He determines that he needs a car but can manage with an inexpensive one, one that costs only $20,000. However, he wants, and does buy, a $50,000 car. He then owes Ḥuqúq on the difference, 19 per cent of $30,000.

None of the above people would be wrong in their choices. In fact, *all are right*, if they prayed about their decisions and followed their consciences.

Something I find quite amazing about Ḥuqúqu'lláh

is that it is *only* 19 per cent. Once a person's needs are met, why does God not ask for *all* of the surplus? Allowing us to keep 81 per cent says to me that we have a most generous Father.

A reminder: Payment of Ḥuqúqu'lláh holds the highest priority. As you consider your contributions towards Bahá'í funds and non-Bahá'í charities, remember the following:

> Contributions to the funds of the Faith cannot be considered as part of one's payment of Ḥuqúqu'lláh; moreover, if one owes Ḥuqúqu'lláh and cannot afford both to pay it and to make contributions to the Fund, the payment of Ḥuqúqu'lláh should take priority over making contributions. But as to whether contributions to the Fund may be treated as expenses in calculating the amount of one's assets on which Ḥuqúqu'lláh, is payable; this is left to the judgement of each individual in the light of his own circumstances.[5]

Simplify, Simplify

> To live simply,
> so that others may simply live.
> *Gandhi*

This book's motto of simplicity applies to finances too. When you uncomplicate your financial life as much as you can, you make more room for tranquillity. Consider the following:

How widespread are your debts? Having too many debts can be fatiguing and stressful. If you have a number of loans outstanding it might be time to consolidate them. But not at any cost. The interest rates on consolidation loans vary greatly, so shop carefully.

Put as many bills as possible on direct payment. The phone bill, the gas bill and so on can be paid automatically from your bank account every month. Running around to pay bills in person is a conspicuous waste of time.

Arrange for investments (e.g. monthly retirement savings) to be automatically deducted from your account monthly.

Reduce your credit cards to one or two. More are just

unnecessary complications in your life. No one needs a different card for each store. If you acquired an extra card because you got a discount on your purchases if you used the store's own card, then that was a prudent decision the day you bought new furniture. Now cut up the store's card and return to using your one chosen credit card. This keeps bill-paying simple.

Always pay your credit card bill in full every month. Unable to? Is your interest climbing? Perhaps you're not ready yet to use a credit card responsibly and should continue to use cash or a debit card for now.

Financial simplicity necessitates staying organized. When we discussed having personal files in chapter 7, 'Your Home Office', a number of files were designated for financial records. Using these files has a direct bearing on your time management, not to mention your sanity. If you need to return a new pair of shoes because the heel fell off the second time you wore them, do you know exactly where to find that receipt in your home? Did you start a 'Receipts: temporary' file? Is the receipt somewhere in the paper pile on your desk? Maybe it went out with last week's rubbish? Can you sit down to prepare your annual tax return efficiently because everything is filed in one place or does it take you longer to gather the raw materials than it does to actually fill out the forms?

Spend time with a professional financial planner. Once a year is good for most people, more if your circumstances dictate it. A financial planner will help you keep your investments and actions in line with your objectives. Are you saving enough each month to retire when you intend to?

If you want to do your own on-line trading, have your eyes wide open – not only to the intricacies of the stock market but also to the true costs involved, namely your time. If it requires half an hour a day for you to stay current (and many people spend *hours* a day), are you getting true value for your time? Are you making substantial profits that are worth that amount of time? If not, either admit that this activity primarily serves an entertainment purpose for you or else choose some well-performing mutual funds or term deposits and get on with your life.

> Our life is frittered away by detail . . . Simplify, simplify.
> Let your affairs be as two or three, and not a hundred
> or a thousand;
> instead of a million, count half a dozen
> and keep your accounts on your thumbnail.
> *Thoreau*

Wills

Unto everyone hath been enjoined the writing of a will. The testator should head this document with the adornment of the Most Great Name, bear witness therein unto the oneness of God in the Dayspring of His Revelation, and make mention, as he may wish, of that which is praiseworthy, so that it may be a testimony for him in the kingdoms of Revelation and Creation and a treasure with his Lord, the Supreme Protector, the Faithful.[6]

A will is an essential element of good life management. It is also mandatory for Bahá'ís, as we see above. Not to have a will is just plain selfish. Not having a will is usually due to procrastination or avoidance of contemplating one's own mortality. Not writing a will doesn't make you invincible or keep you young. And not writing a will doesn't mean you won't need one.

Dying without having prepared a will is not going to be a problem for *you* because you'll be dead. Rather, your missing will leaves a mess for other people to clean up. Grieving your passing is challenging enough for your loved ones; they do not need the additional legal burden of you having died intestate.

Many people with basic assets draft their own wills, using a how-to book. This is not difficult and it is legal in many countries. I wrote my own will. Other people need or prefer the assistance of a lawyer. Whatever your method, if you have not yet prepared your will . . . Just Do It! Put 'Prepare my will' as an urgent item on your 'To Do' list . . . *Now.*

Bahá'í Wills

Bahá'ís draft their wills much the same as other people do but a Bahá'í will also includes:

- the Greatest Name symbol at the top of the page
- a declaration that the author of the will is a follower of Bahá'u'lláh, as cited above ('bear witness therein unto the oneness of God in the Dayspring of His Revelation')
- instructions for a Bahá'í funeral and burial. You may simply say 'Bahá'í funeral and burial in accor-

dance with Bahá'í law' or list the specifics if you so choose, such as from what materials you want your casket made. In some countries the will is not read until after the funeral, so you might need to make your wishes for the funeral and burial known in some other way.

The necessary wording of wills varies from place to place and country to country. Even the laws regarding wills and inheritance are subject to periodic changes, so consult the current guidelines where you live or hire a lawyer to assist in the preparation of your will.

Testaments

I encourage you to consider including a testament. The 'testament' part of one's 'Will and Testament' is often forgotten by people writing their wills. People think of a will as being a 'who-gets-what list' and forget to make their closing statements to the world.

A testament can be a beautiful thing. It is your opportunity to tell the people present at the reading of your will who Bahá'u'lláh is and why you followed His teachings. You can include words of love and encouragement to the people you love. You can complain about the price of coffee if that's what's important to you. Say anything you like but do say something! This is *your* last testament.

11

Retirement

Sooner or later I am going to die,
but I am not going to retire.
Margaret Mead

Somewhere in western culture the word 'work' became
a dirty word. 'Don't work too hard!' friends joke with
each other. People complain about work and live for the
weekend. Why *not* work hard, be highly productive and
give your best to the world around you? People who
find value in their work are happier people outside of
work too.

Work done in the spirit of service
is the highest form of worship . . .
'Abdu'l-Bahá[1]

When work is regarded as the enemy, then retirement is
seen as the imaginary saviour. Retirement becomes one
big weekend to look forward to. Sleeping in every
morning, golfing every afternoon. Alas, people with this
attitude are usually disappointed. This type of retirement is fun for a while, until the apathy sets in. The
highest rate of new-onset depression is found amongst

The quality of life in retirement has
never looked so good

men who have retired within the past two years. Making a contribution and feeling valued is essential to mental and emotional well-being.

> I never think of myself as retired.
> Retirement to me means inactivity.
> I do most certainly believe in a change of activity
> when it becomes time for what is commonly called
> retirement.
> *J.C. Penney*

Ever wonder where the idea of 'retirement' came from? It hasn't been around forever. In fact, it is a relatively new concept. People used to start families in their late teens and worked hard all day hunting, gathering and surviving. Then, if they were lucky, they lived to the ripe old age of 34. Working for all of one's life, albeit a short one, has been the norm until very recent history.

Government Pensions

In 1889 Germany implemented the first social programme of financial support for its elderly citizens. It was a compassionate measure that relieved people of the burden of working in extreme old age. At that time the average life expectancy was 45 years. The age at which they chose to start a pension programme was 65. It was a far-off age that few people attained. Supporting the occasional few who did live that long did not pose any notable financial burden on the state.

Other nations gradually adopted similar policies, also using the distant 65 as the age of retirement. In Canada, for example, when its Old Age Pension Act

came into being in 1927, the average life expectancy
was 60 years. Today it is 76 years for men and 80 for
women, yet the standard age for retirement remains at
65 nearly worldwide. This means people are spending
an increasing number of years in retirement.

Many governments would like to raise the age at
which people are eligible for a senior's pension, simply
based on the maths cited above. Despite the logic of
such a move, it remains highly unpopular for any government to attempt to implement, especially amongst
64-year-old voters!

I'm not going to enter the argument of whether or
not countries and corporations should raise the age of
retirement. There are passionate and persuasive arguments on both sides. It does cause us to ponder though
– why are we living longer and has the quality of our
lives improved?

Living Longer, Living Better?

There is no doubt that medical advances have greatly
extended the human lifespan. We have drastically
reduced the rate of infant mortality. We are better able
to treat disease. We have developed surgical techniques
that save and prolong lives. We now know more about
the merits of hygiene, nutrition and exercise. The
quality of life in retirement has never looked so good!

When I was a young child I remember meeting my
maternal grandmother for the first time. She was old by
my six-year-old standards (late 50s), was slightly overweight and walked with a slow shuffle. She was no
different from my playmates' grandmothers. They were
all old grannies in their 50s. Today, by comparison,

there are many 60-year-old grandmothers who are lean and agile, love their work and have no plans to stop. While the traditional retirement *age* may not have changed, what the word retirement *means* to people certainly has.

What does retirement mean to you? If you are going to live for 75 or a hundred years, what kind of shape do you want to be in, physically and financially? A sentiment expressed by many regretful seniors is 'If I'd known I was going to live this long I'd have taken better care of myself!'

Retirement as a Beginning, Not an End

> You should retire only when
> you can find something you enjoy doing
> more than what you are doing now.
> *George Burns*

Seniors who have planned wisely view retirement as a new period of productivity. The only difference now is that there is less importance placed on receiving financial reward from their daily activities. Through pensions, investments or by living with their children, these retirees are not stressed over the necessity of earning a living as they may have been at an earlier time in their lives. They remain active people but making money is less important. This can be a very liberating period of life.

Some people of retirement age continue with paid employment to supplement their pension incomes. A retiree might continue to work without pay purely to mentor the next generation of craftsmen learning the skills the retiree has mastered. Some work full- or part-time without pay for charitable causes. Many retirees enjoy caring for their grandchildren while their own children are off contributing to the busy wheels of the economy. Having a sense of purpose is a mandatory element of a happy retirement, whether or not one receives financial compensation for one's contribution.

> It can be a delight to a man
> who comes at last to a well-earned job
> instead of a well-earned rest.
> *Wilder Penfield*

Bahá'ís in Retirement

Most references in the Bahá'í writings which use the word retirement use it in the context of its second meaning in the Oxford dictionary – 'to withdraw, to retreat', as when referring to Bahá'u'lláh's two-year retirement to the mountains of Kurdistan during His exile. The Kitáb-i-Aqdas, the Bahá'í book of laws, does not prescribe a certain age at which a Bahá'í should 'give up one's regular work because of advancing age', the primary definition listed by Oxford. As for a set age for retirement, the Bahá'í writings only say the following:

> Concerning the retirement from work for individuals who have reached a certain age, Shoghi Effendi in a letter written on his behalf stated that 'this is a matter on which the International House of Justice will have to legislate as there are no provisions in the Aqdas concerning it'.[2]

The freedom to pioneer is the reward of many Bahá'ís who retire. If they had been wanna-be pioneers until now, this is the time they do it. Whether they move to another continent or to a village just 20 kilometres away, the retirees are able to fulfil a *vital* need of the Faith.

While the Aqdas does exempt people from fasting after the age of 70, it does not say that a Bahá'í should stop *serving* the Faith at any certain age. You might retire from your chosen profession but you don't retire from being a Bahá'í. Many Bahá'ís in retirement say they are too busy serving the Cause for retirement boredom and depression to grab hold of them. As one Bahá'í retiree put it, 'My purpose in life has never been so clear and retirement now affords me more time to give to the Cause. This is the most exhilarating time in my life!'

Having a sense of purpose insulates people from post-retirement blues. The Bahá'ís I have observed and interviewed who have retired from their primary employment, and who remain active within the Bahá'í community, appear more joyful than average retirees. They travel teach. They pioneer. They mentor Bahá'í youth. They serve their communities in countless ways. They are too engaged in life to be depressed! They have a sense of purpose.

> I would rather wear out than rust out.
> *Kemmons Wilson*

If You Must Work . . .

If through poor planning or poor luck you find yourself unable to retire at the age that others around you are, do not despair. If you need to continue working to support yourself later in life, you are in good company. Many people feel that a senior's pension alone is insufficient and continue working well into their 80s, if only part-time. Their minds and bodies remain more youthful than their contemporaries because they do not allow others to tell them how elderly people 'should' behave.

12

Time Management for Bahá'í Administration

Gaining Administrative Experience

The average Bahá'í is more likely to acquire administrative experience than the average person who is not a Bahá'í. Generally, people gain their administrative skills through holding a managerial position at work or through community volunteer service. In addition to sometimes having these roles in life, Bahá'ís also acquire administrative skills through their Bahá'í service. It is uncommon to make it through one's entire Bahá'í life without being called upon, at some time or another, to serve at some level of the Bahá'í administration. You might be appointed to a committee, be elected to a Local or National Assembly or be appointed an assistant to an Auxiliary Board member. A few souls are even called upon to serve as Board members, Counsellors or as members of the Universal House of Justice.

The experience gained through Bahá'í administrative service is a gift Bahá'ís can extend to the world around them. You might be the only person to serve on a new committee in your workplace who has experience of chairing a meeting or taking minutes. You can offer these skills to the group. If your colleagues ask how you acquired such skills, this is an opportunity for you to briefly say something about the Bahá'í Faith.

You are likely to be the only Bahá'í on your committee at work and therefore be the only one accustomed to Bahá'í consultation. This can be a struggle for many Bahá'ís. Sitting in a meeting where people talk at the same time, raise their voices, even deliberately try to dominate each other and do not support decisions outside of the meeting can be a painful test of patience for a Bahá'í.

The encouragement I give Bahá'ís in this position is 'Hang in there!' Resist the urge to give up and walk away in despair. You cannot change a corporate culture overnight, just as Bahá'u'lláh's new world order did not manifest itself throughout the world the day He declared His mission. Good things take time. Keep your candle burning and don't complain about how dark the meeting room still is. Your light will eventually spread to others. The courtesy you show when you speak, the flair you demonstrate if you're chairing, the respect you show when listening to others, not getting drawn into loud debates, *is* being noticed by others, even if you feel your efforts are futile.

Your job is not your primary purpose in life. It doesn't matter if your committee at work makes mistakes and takes the long road to its goals. Your purpose is to be a Bahá'í in whatever setting you happen to be. One by one there will be more 'candles' willing to practise Bahá'í consultation because they recognize its merits.

You need not introduce your style as 'Bahá'í consultation' to your colleagues. That could make some people resistant if they are concerned you're about to push your religion at work. Bahá'í consultation is good consultation by whatever name it gets introduced. Simply suggest to your colleagues the techniques you want the group to consider using, such as speaking in turn, not repeating something said, detaching oneself from one's own contribution, following the chairperson and so on. The ideas can be presented gradually if it would be too great a reversal to implement them at once.

When a new committee or task force is appointed at work, during the first meeting you might ask by what ground rules everyone wants to operate. If asked with some humour, 'For example, shall we all talk at the same time or shall we listen to each other in turn?' people see how silly the comparison is and the best choice is obvious. If a chairperson is not appointed for the first meeting, offer to chair that meeting yourself. You can outline respectful consultation techniques at the outset and proceed with gentle leadership. This will set a style for whoever takes on the regular task of chairing.

Why is there so much emphasis on consultation in a time management book? *A group consulting with respect and courtesy functions more efficiently.* You don't waste time repeating yourselves. If people feel listened to the first time, they won't react and defend their points again later. When harmony and goodwill are felt by all the group members, the group's goals are more readily achieved.

Throughout this chapter the term 'Assembly' is used but most of the information is also applicable to committees and task forces. The techniques espoused in this chapter will make any Bahá'í administrative service more efficient and less stressful.

Mentorship

Bahá'ís are at various individual levels of experience and expertise. When someone is elected onto an Assembly for the first time, she can feel quite nervous going into her first Assembly meeting, especially if the other members have had previous Assembly experience. Not knowing the process of Assembly meetings leaves the newcomer feeling disadvantaged.

The veteran Assembly members will warmly welcome the newcomer and explain a few basics to her. From there on it's teaching by example. The newcomer will quickly learn how an Assembly operates by mere observation. The skills required to participate in the meetings will be learned through the example of others – actively listening, waiting one's turn to speak, staying on topic, not displaying passion and so on.

When someone does go off topic, it is the tactful job of the chair to lovingly bring that person back to the subject. It is so easy for our thoughts to be led astray by an exciting idea passing through our minds. When we are impressed with our own brilliant ideas, sometimes the thoughts leap out of our mouths before we assess whether it is even an appropriate moment to speak. Every Assembly member has the responsibility to pay attention to the discussion. Catching oneself almost jumping in – and off the topic! – is both an entertaining and educational/humbling experience. Other Assembly members can assist the chair by pointing out when the group has gone astray, for the chair might not catch every occurrence.

Administration is a Growth Opportunity

I once had a very humbling experience. I was frustrated with a committee that did a poor job of organizing an evening meeting for a special guest coming to our city to speak. The task was easy. They would appoint a master of ceremonies for the evening, choose some writings and music, ask a few people to bring refreshments and so on – a straightforward public meeting, as done so many times in our city.

The night of the event arrived. The room looked lovely, accented with flowers and candles. Lots of delicious food was ready in the kitchen. People gathered and sat in their seats. Then everyone waited. And waited. Nothing happened. It was getting late. Nervously, I slunk over to the chairperson of the committee to ask what the hold-up was.

'What are we waiting for?' I asked.

'Nothing, I guess,' was the reply.

'Can the programme please start?'

'Okay.'

'So where is your M.C.?'

Pause.

'We don't have one. I guess we forgot that.'

In disbelief I whispered, 'Then please get up there yourself to welcome everyone and introduce the programme! The audience is waiting!'

I think I missed the rest of the event despite sitting in the front row. I was too busy in my mind judging the errors of the evening as they unfolded. An improper introduction here, poor timing there. It was an inexcusably sloppy show, I thought. I vented to a fellow Assembly member later during the car ride home.

'This was a simple meeting to plan! How could they possibly miss something so obvious as a M.C.? The Assembly gave clear instructions what the expectations were for the evening! How could they screw it up so badly?'

My friend paused. I dread such pauses. They are usually followed by some wise words that point out my foolish ways. This time was no exception.

'You know, Catherine,' he said, 'you don't always do what you're supposed to do either.'

The remark hit me like a bucket of ice water.

'You could have arranged this evening's gathering to glowing perfection. That's probably why it wasn't tasked to you. It's someone else's turn to learn. You, however, could be working on a strategy for our Assembly to achieve its Plan goals. Look how far behind the Assembly is on this job.'

He was so right. I considered their task easy but it wasn't easy for them. There were individuals on that committee who could plan a children's class with no notice at all. I, however, could struggle ineptly for days trying to plan a children's class and still not do it well.

In Bahá'í administration we will sometimes feel our abilities are stretched. Mentoring is part of Assembly and committee service. New members will learn from their veteran colleagues and later go on to become mentors for other newcomers to Bahá'í administration.

Meeting Times

There is no right or wrong time to hold an Assembly meeting. Evening, daytime, weekends – they all are fine, depending on the schedules of your members. Many

National Assemblies and Local Assemblies with large communities lean towards holding meetings that last for two or three days, often over a weekend, because their agendas are extensive and one evening doesn't suffice.

No matter what time of day your meeting is held, be sure it starts *on time*. If your Assembly routinely starts late, with people arriving at the time the meeting should begin or later, the people who tend to arrive late will continue to do so. 'The meeting doesn't start until quarter past the hour anyway, so I'm okay arriving a little late,' they rationalize. But if the meeting always starts on time with prayers, those who have a tendency to run late will soon be arriving on time.

The same holds true for Nineteen Day Feasts. Earn a reputation for your Feasts always starting on time and the problem of late arrivals will noticeably diminish. Having devotions interrupted by latecomers can be a concern at Feasts. Where the location of the Feast permits, many communities do not allow people to walk into the room in the middle of devotions. Instead, latecomers wait in another room or foyer and enter only when a brief break in the programme permits. Potentially missing part of the devotions is an incentive to arrive on time. (Review the section on 'Punctuality'.)

Punctuality at Assembly meetings includes ending on time. If your meeting is scheduled to end at 5:00 p.m., then do so. The other items carry forward to the next meeting. Knowing the meeting will end on time helps Assembly members keep themselves in check. 'Do I really have to speak? Was my comment already said?' Refraining from unnecessary speech is a responsible contribution to consultation and staying on time.

'They won't be late next time!'

The habit of being long-winded is easier to self-monitor when the time allotted for each item is known. Some Assemblies give themselves a time limit for each agenda item. It is even written into the agenda. Of course, the best laid plans can change. An item that the secretary thought would easily result in agreement and was allotted ten minutes on the agenda could create a clash of ideas requiring more lengthy consultation. When this happens, the chair must decide if it is worth sacrificing something else on today's agenda to continue with this topic or to table the item for another meeting.

No agenda should be so tight that the slightest deviation stresses the chairperson. Build flexitime into the agenda. It will absorb unexpected long consultations, as well as allow for necessary breaks for humour.

During one Assembly meeting we all sat around one large table and lit candles to add ambience to the room. At one point I turned the page of my agenda and inadvertently set it afire in a candle. A few jokes were made as we patted out the flame, then carried on with the meeting. Moments later I excused myself to go the washroom. I assumed my honourable colleagues would continue the consultation in my brief absence. Not so. They were in a playful mood. When I returned to the room, I saw a fire extinguisher beside my chair and a large jug of water at my place at the table. 'Just in case!' they said.

Starting Your Meetings

Here is 'Abdu'l-Bahá's guidance on consultation:

The first condition is absolute love and harmony amongst the members of the assembly. They must be wholly free from estrangement and must manifest in themselves the Unity of God, for they are the waves of one sea, the drops of one river, the stars of one heaven, the rays of one sun, the trees of one orchard, the flowers of one garden.[1]

Being in perfect love and harmony with eight other people you didn't hand-pick yourself can be a challenge. An interesting variety of personalities can be brought together at election time. Is perfect love and harmony possible? It is certainly a worthy goal. Perfection aside, even with *good* love and harmony an Assembly can function well.

A technique that helps many Assemblies and committees build love and unity is to start meetings by getting to know each other better. Each member takes one minute to update the others on what is going on in his life. This enables the members to know one another more intimately, build friendships and thereby become more understanding. During one sharing time I learned that an Assembly colleague was facing a difficult health problem. This enabled me to be more patient whenever that member failed to complete some of his assigned tasks before the next meeting. Many times I have thought, 'Wow. I didn't know that about you' during the sharing segment of meetings. Without this sharing time I wouldn't know and appreciate so much about my colleagues.

Sharing about ourselves sets a peaceful tone to a meeting. So does deepening. By reading a quotation from the writings and discussing it for a while has a spiritual effect upon the members. It reminds everyone

why they are there. Focusing on the holy word recon-
nects us to our purpose of serving Bahá'u'lláh.

Dealing with Estrangement

From time to time Bahá'ís will become annoyed with
the actions, lack of actions, words said, words not said,
of each other. An Auxiliary Board member I know
gives the following advice to Bahá'ís who have criti-
cisms of themselves, others or even the Institutions of
the Faith: 'The only Bahá'ís who aren't making any
mistakes are the ones who aren't doing anything.' How
true. Go ahead, make a few mistakes. And overlook the
shortcomings of others too. No one of us is perfect. As
long as we are ardently giving the best we can to this
Cause we love so much, God will see a way to make all
things right.

Sometimes estrangement can become serious.
During one Assembly meeting it seemed that there was
tension between two members. Their comments after
each other's contributions seemed accusatory. Finally
another member said, 'What's going on between you
two?'

'Nothing,' was the answer.

'Something is going on and I'm very uncomfortable
with the tone of this meeting. It's tense in here. We
need to discuss this tension before we can move on.'

Feathers began to fly. The two individuals, who used
to be close friends, revealed that their personal friendship was on the line and they refused to speak to each
other outside of Assembly meetings. The other
Assembly members were completely unaware this had
been going on. But this explained the pattern of some

difficult Assembly meetings that had recently taken place.

Our kind and loving chair shared these words: 'As long as there is estrangement between members of this Assembly we cannot proceed with consulting on community matters. The requisite love and harmony isn't in place. Friends, the Assembly needs to lovingly and frankly help these two souls heal their relationship. Only then can we continue with our agenda.'

A hush fell over the room. We all knew the chairperson was right. We also all knew how many urgent items were on the agenda. 'Can't we deal with some of our *really* urgent items and fix this personal problem next meeting?' was the angst showing on some faces but which no one dared to express. Before we could truly experience Bahá'í consultation, the love and unity of our membership had to be secured. Theoretically we knew that. But here we were being tested. We were confronted with the challenge of discarding our urgent agenda to focus on re-establishing Assembly unity.

For the next two hours the Assembly heard the concerns of these two estranged friends and consulted on the matter. At times it was painful. At the end of the two hours the situation was somewhat improved, though the friendship was not yet healed. The Assembly unanimously agreed who would provide ongoing counselling for these two friends. After this consultation everyone was emotionally exhausted. No other matters were consulted upon. But what would become of the urgent items? I firmly believe that when you follow Bahá'u'lláh's way, He truly helps you out.

On that agenda was a request from an interfaith organization to appoint a Bahá'í to its board. We later learned that their next meeting was postponed, giving us another month to consult on the appointment. Our teaching committee, which urgently wanted the Assembly's feedback on a proposed project, the next day withdrew its request in order to make more elaborate plans. Somehow the urgency of those and other agenda items disappeared!

Agenda Preparation

All meetings function best when the agenda is prepared and circulated in advance. Having all the Assembly members show up and say, 'So what shall we discuss today?' is a colossal waste of time. Everyone, not just the chair and secretary, can contribute to agenda preparation. Here's how:

Give the items you know are for the agenda to the chair and secretary long before the meeting is held. Springing 'This is urgent and has to be discussed today!' at the start of a meeting is not appreciated, if it could have appeared in the prepared agenda ahead of time.

Be acquainted with the minutes from the previous meeting *before* going to the current meeting. Correcting and approving the minutes can be swift if everyone present is prepared. If one person waits to read his copy of the minutes *during* the meeting, it holds everyone up. Your Assembly can only move as fast as its slowest member.

Be prepared with the relevant writings for your agenda items. Assemblies that turn to the writings and not their members' individual beliefs report a noticeable calm and effectiveness in their work. You can't research every agenda item but you can bring to the meeting the writings for the items *you* put on the agenda. When possible, circulate the writings to your colleagues by email beforehand so they have time to pray, meditate and prepare for the meeting.

Agenda Formats

The format used in agenda preparation influences the efficiency of the consultation. An effective technique used by experienced secretaries is to turn the agenda items into *questions*. Compare these two agendas:

Agenda A:
    1. Bahá'í Centre
        a. Kitchen
        b. Keys
        c. Pictures
    2. Feast Committee
        a. Membership
        b. Mandate
        c. Budget

Agenda B:
    1. Bahá'í Centre
        a. Kitchen sink leaking. Know a good plumber?
        b. How many keys have been copied and who has them? Who should have copies?
        c. Artwork is needed for the lobby. Suggestions?
    2. Feast Committee
        a. Needs two more members. Who shall we appoint?

    b. What items should appear in their mandate we are drafting today?

    c. What should be their budget for the next Bahá'í year?

Notice how the second agenda more clearly states the issues. An agenda presented in the form of questions causes the Assembly members to think in the form of *answers*. They come to the meeting better prepared for consultation. The first agenda tells the reader that something is going on regarding the sink and some keys. With the second agenda, the LSA members are able to think about plumbers they've met, if they have spare keys to the Centre or to which committees the keys have been loaned.

Even if you cannot circulate the final agenda until the start of the meeting, questions still help members consult more effectively. They will be better focused on the topics.

Hijacking an Assembly Meeting

How does an Assembly choose the priority subjects for its consultations? If your agenda seems to have 16 hours' worth of consultation in it but you are only meeting for three hours tonight, choosing which items will get your attention can be a challenge.

One way, and not the best way, is for an Assembly to let its agendas be externally driven. They respond to crisis after crisis, urgency after urgency. This means they fall victim to anxious community members (or committees) who want an answer to their issue NOW. It may well be urgent, in the mind of the person bringing the matter to the Assembly, but often the matter could have been handled a different way.

Example: Joe has written a pamphlet and he wants to print 500 copies before he goes on a travel teaching trip this weekend. He gives the draft to Richard, an Assembly member, one hour before the Assembly meeting. Joe asks if it could be approved tonight. He is relieved that he 'got it in on time'. This can be likened to giving your accountant a box full of receipts the evening before your income tax is due and thinking you have met the deadline.

Before the Assembly can approve this pamphlet its members (all or an appointed few) will need to read it. To do so during the meeting is improper use of Assembly consultation time. That's the kind of preparation work that should happen outside of the actual Assembly meeting. (If you think this 'fictitious' story is an obvious example of having unrealistic expectations of one's Assembly, I regretfully inform you that Assemblies are unfortunately faced with situations like this all too frequently.)

Let's say Richard read the draft before the Assembly meeting started, as it is always his habit to arrive early. And let's say the Assembly actually does fit in a few minutes to discuss this pamphlet, since the Assembly prioritizes teaching initiatives.

'Is it well written?' asks the chair.

'Some of it concerns me,' says Richard and he reads a part of the text aloud.

The Assembly unanimously agrees that the pamphlet in principle is good. It is also clear that parts of it are poorly written. It cannot be quickly remedied during this Assembly meeting. The Assembly decides to thank Joe for his initiative in producing teaching materials, encouraging him to ask other community members with good editing skills to proofread for him in the future. The Assembly is unable to approve this particular brochure by Joe's deadline and regretfully must advise him to use brochures the teaching committee already has in stock.

Joe had known of his travel teaching trip for three months. He procrastinated in writing his pamphlet, causing his last minute rush to get it to the Assembly. Had Joe submitted a draft a few weeks earlier, a revised version would likely have been printed in time.

This is an example of 'external sources' hijacking an Assembly meeting. An external source is anything the Assembly did not put on its agenda in keeping with its overall goals for the community. External source items are good. They show that individual initiatives are thriving. However, to have Assembly meetings dominated by smaller 'urgent' external source items and sacrificing the greater planning for which an Assembly is responsible shows *the Assembly is not in control of its agenda.*

An Assembly does not have a blank agenda. The chair does not start the meetings with, 'What shall we do today? Has anyone in the community brought us something to do?' Assemblies are proactive. They lead the community! There is usually a full agenda.

Assembly members can be heartbroken when the Assembly is not able to address an issue as urgently as a community member wants. The loving parent wants to respond to all its community members' initiatives and problems promptly. Community members might not be aware of the volume or intensity of many of the

Assembly's matters. Loving support for the Assembly meeting and its agenda should be *everyone's* concern, for it is everyone's Assembly.

I heard a Bahá'í state that *when an Assembly is meeting, it is the most important event in that community* – more important than the Prime Minister visiting your city, more important than the hockey play-offs. During Assembly meetings, she prays at home for them. After prayer, she goes about her tasks in loving awareness that God's guidance is being infused into her community. What a mature attitude!

Urgent vs. Important, Assembly Style

Any active Assembly has a number of urgent items on its agenda. But how much of its agenda is *important*? There is a huge difference between urgent and important. An important item could be raising community awareness of a fund prioritized by the Universal House of Justice. An urgent item could be that the stereo was stolen from the Bahá'í Centre. Urgent items always appear with flags waving and sirens wailing, begging 'deal with me now'! Important items are often not so loud, patiently waiting their turn. Important items can usually be deferred to the next meeting because 'today we have urgent items to discuss'. At the next meeting the important items can be deferred once again, and on it goes.

Sometimes an item is both urgent and important. 'The local news channel wants to interview one of us tomorrow about the significance of the Festival of Riḍván!' Urgent, important items such as this have no trouble getting the Assembly's attention. Safeguarding consultation time for the important, non-urgent agenda items is the challenging assignment set before Assemblies.

The Teaching Priority

Do you ever have trouble knowing where to start on your agenda? Allow the Universal House of Justice to make that decision easier for you:

> And since the primary purpose for which Local Spiritual Assemblies are established is to promote the teaching work, it is clear that every National Spiritual Assembly must give careful consideration to ways and means to encourage each Local Assembly under its jurisdiction to fulfil its principal obligation . . .[2]

Assemblies that shift their agendas to ensure that teaching remains their priority report greater satisfaction with their meetings. Janice tells of how her Assembly changed its focus:

> We felt like we were working so hard and not going anywhere. The faster we went, the more behind we got. It was depressing. Then at the start of one meeting we deepened on the quote by the House of Justice that tells Assemblies to put teaching first. So we did. We ensured teaching would be the top agenda item at each meeting. It was a struggle at first. There were always urgent items that seemed more pressing at the time but we stuck to our plan and discussed teaching before anything else.
>
> It transformed our meetings! We went home with a feeling of accomplishment and that our community was headed in the right direction. We didn't tackle everything

on our agenda but at least we felt like we did what was most important. At the end of the year we wanted to be able to say we did what was truly most important to Bahá'u'lláh.

Timing and Courtesy

Sometimes Assembly members get excited about an issue and speak without the chair's acknowledgement. If jumping in is the only way you will get your turn, then your Assembly needs to stop consulting on the agenda items completely. It's time to go back and deepen on how to consult.

A useful technique to combat jumping in is for everyone to agree to pause between speakers. Before starting in with your comment, no matter how clever you think it is, pause. Allow a few seconds of silence between speakers. A few seconds goes a long way. This practice can actually transform your Assembly's consultative atmosphere! Pausing assures members that everyone is truly listening and reflecting on the contribution just made, rather than people just giving a quick retort. You feel like you're actually *consulting*. Bahá'ís who discover the technique of pausing say it is a humbling revelation of their own urgency to speak.

For this to work, good chairmanship is required. The chair must note who wants to make a contribution. When the friends have trust in the chair they won't be on the edges of their seats trying to get their comments in.

Pausing also helps everyone stay on topic. An off-topic comment is more likely to be said on impulse and not done intentionally. If a dear colleague does stray, it is the responsibility of the chair to lovingly bring him back into focus.

> Chair: We want to increase the number of Bahá'í books in the public library. Any suggestions? Do we even know what titles we have there?

> Nasim: I think there's one copy each of *Gleanings* and *Some Answered Questions* at the main branch.

> Mark: Is that all?

> Nasim: The last time I checked was during the Riḍván Festival when we had that booth set up in the library lobby. They only had those two books on file then.

> Bert: That reminds me . . . that Riḍván display is sitting the storage room in the Bahá'í Centre basement. Other boxes of stuff have been thrown in there since and the beautiful pictures on that display are getting wrecked. We've got to take better care of our display materials. Where else can we put them?

> Chair: Bert, we're discussing the library books right now. Do you want 'Storage of displays' added to the agenda?

> Bert: Oops. Yes, please.

Skilful chairmanship kept the Assembly on topic and politely let Bert know he had strayed. Everyone slips from time to time. Had Bert paused for a few seconds, however, he would have been more likely to notice that his comment was off topic.

Adopting a new consultation technique, like pausing, can help an Assembly bond. It is a new skill you've agreed to work on together. If everyone has to wait three full seconds before speaking, fewer errors of speech occur. At times it is fun, as you smile at each other during the silences or catch each other when you accidentally change the subject. Make a game of it. He who fouls the most serves the others tea.

Introduce pausing at your next Assembly meeting. Don't be surprised if its influence is profound!

13

Administrative Efficiency

This chapter contains MORE time management strategies for Bahá'í administrative service. Here we examine the nitty-gritty details that help Bahá'í Assemblies function more efficiently.

Getting Things Done

An Assembly that feels it consults well and makes a lot of good decisions for the community can still have problems actually getting things done. Looking at the Assembly minutes, one might assume that everything is unfolding perfectly in that community. In reality, though, not all of the decisions reported in the minutes are executed. People forget tasks assigned to them, they get too busy or their attention is usurped by a new urgent item. Here are some methods to improve your Assembly's follow-through on its decisions:

Have a tracking system for your decisions. At each meeting read your minutes from the previous meeting and ask if the tasks were done. 'Item 4.2, Children's classes. We need a teacher for the preschool age group. Decision: ask Maria Degara to teach the preschool class for the remainder of this term. Action: Ricardo.

Ricardo, was this done?' If Ricardo says he forgot or that Maria is out of town until tomorrow, enter this decision in a log kept by one of your Assembly members. If Ricardo is not present at the meeting to answer, enter it in the log. At each meeting your outstanding 'to do' items will be inquired about until they are completed.

If a long gap occurs between your meetings, use a system for informing each other of your tasks done, such as by email. If you were tasked with buying a new fax machine for the Assembly, email your Assembly colleagues to tell them your task has been completed, as agreed upon. When your colleagues are up to date on the follow-through of all Assembly decisions, they can better respond to questions from community members. They can also assist you if you hit an obstacle.

Give your committees clear mandates or terms of reference. Every member of a committee should have a written copy. By clearly outlining what is expected of it, the committee can forge ahead with its responsibilities. Often, knowing what is *not* its area of responsibility is just as important. If an item is not in its mandate, the committee is not responsible for it. Other people in the community are looking after those affairs. Recommend that every committee periodically reviews its mandate. It is the compass that guides it. A sample mandate follows:

Feast Committee Mandate

1. To plan, organize and assure the regular celebration of Nineteen Day Feasts in our community.

2. To prepare readings for the devotional portion of each Nineteen Day Feast. Consult with your Assembly liaison when the Assembly requests the readings complement a specific consultation topic.

3. To invite and schedule hosts for refreshments for the social part of the Feasts.

4. To assure an appropriate spiritual and devotional ambiance through the careful arrangement of lighting, furniture and decorations.

5. To assure the quality of the devotions through the careful selection of readers and chanters whose contributions will enhance the spirituality of the Feast.

6. To prepare the Feast programme to involve the arts, as appropriate, in the context of specific Feast topics.

7. To assure that children are welcome guests at the Feast through participation in the devotional programme.

8. To propose an annual budget for the committee for approval by the Assembly and to maintain control over expenditures.

9. To forward minutes of your meetings to the Assembly and liaison member via email as soon as possible after each meeting.

10. To refer to the Committee Resource Package for

guidelines on general functions and responsibilities of committees, including guidelines for consultation.

11. To refer to the Committee Resource Package for the roles and responsibilities of the committee's chair, secretary and treasurer, as well as the Assembly liaison.

12. To submit an annual report to the Assembly by 1 April of each year.

Notes:

a. Include at least one piece of music at the beginning and another piece later in the devotional programme.

b. Please select prayers and readings from the writings of the Báb, Bahá'u'lláh and 'Abdu'l-Bahá. Although the holy scriptures of other religions can be used, it is preferable to use the Bábí and Bahá'í writings. Please note that the writings of Shoghi Effendi and letters of the Universal House of Justice cannot be used during the devotional portion of the Feast.

c. If songs are used, the lyrics are to be solely from the writings.

d. The devotional programme is to be 25 to 30 minutes. On occasion the Assembly might change this and your committee will be informed adequately in advance.

e. Please refer to *Stirring of the Spirit* as a resource.

Give your task forces clear instructions. (A task force is temporary and often with a single objective, such as 'to plan this year's Ayyám-i-Há party'. A committee is ongoing, such as one to organize all Nineteen Day Feasts.) *Giving time lines is especially important for task forces.* Beyond being given a mandate to 'plan a Bahá'í youth camp for next August', give them short-term markers to keep them on schedule. 'Report back to the Assembly by 11 May with your initial proposal, including recommendations for budget, location and programme.' Written mandates for task forces help clear any confusion if there is a discrepancy of views later.

Keep a personal 'to do' list in a notebook (paper or electronic) you take to Assembly meetings. Don't wait for the minutes to be circulated or rely on your memory in order to start doing your tasks for the Assembly. Start right away!

Delegating

> We should not only use the brains we have,
> but all that we can borrow.
> *Woodrow Wilson*

Delegate all tasks in which the Assembly need not be directly involved. The caretaker of our Bahá'í centre informed us that a toilet in the women's washroom was broken. This task was beyond his mandated janitorial responsibilities. It was on our agenda as an urgent item. After all, we had dignitaries visiting next week and couldn't have a wet floor. We discussed repairing vs. replacing, hiring a professional vs. having a Bahá'í volunteer do the labour. Eventually the 'grandmother' of the Assembly had her turn to speak. It helps to have the wisdom of someone who has been around a while.

She shook her head and chuckled. 'This is an administrative institution responsible for the spiritual leadership of a large city. I can't believe we are sitting here discussing a *toilet*. Can't this be delegated?'

Oops. She was so right. Within minutes a centre maintenance committee was formed. Four handymen in our community were assigned the task of keeping the centre running. If something needed repair, they were to make it happen. Whether they did the repairs themselves or hired professionals, their expertise was trusted. They were to keep the Assembly informed of the expenses and improvements but the consultation of the details was delegated to *them*.

Delegate all tasks the Assembly need not be directly involved with

Delegation of tasks can be given to individuals too. Need some research done prior to an upcoming Assembly consultation? Assign the research duties to one capable community member. Delegation by an Assembly does far more than just get the work done faster. It allows other Bahá'ís to contribute to the administration of the community. They see that they are vital threads in the web of Bahá'í life.

> Few things help an individual more
> than to place responsibility upon him,
> and to let him know that you trust him.
> *Booker T. Washington*

Assembly Offices or Sub-Committees

'Assembly offices' is not a reference to each Assembly member having his own room with a desk and secretary. Wouldn't that be nice! By 'offices' I mean sub-groups within an Assembly as a means of getting things done efficiently.

Occasionally an Assembly finds itself consulting on an issue that seems to take a disproportionate amount of Assembly time with all nine members involved in the consultation. Yet the item merits some consultation rather than the input of just one person. This is where Assembly offices or sub-committees become useful.

This is how offices work. Two or more members of an Assembly are appointed to deal with matters on behalf of the Assembly. Their decisions are Assembly decisions, as they function as an arm of the Assembly. The chair and secretary, for example, naturally form the Assembly's Office of the Secretariat. They consult with each other on matters such as incoming mail and determine which mail items must go on the agenda for discussion and which can be filed. They can take appropriate actions, such as sending simple correspondence, without first waiting for approval at an Assembly meeting.

An Office of the Treasury or a Finance sub-committee can be formed. Two or three Assembly members (one of course being the treasurer) can consult and make day-to-day financial decisions. If the price tag on a given item is rather high, or if the members of the office hold different views, then the matter comes before the whole Assembly for consultation.

Rachel explains:

Our Assembly has many offices and most of us serve on two offices each. It greatly reduces the amount of time the whole Assembly spends consulting on each item. An office can do the initial legwork and consult amongst its three members. For example, the External Affairs Office recommends to the Assembly which events we should be sending representatives to and who would be appropriate to go. The people in our External Affairs Office are well linked that way in society and we rely on their expertise. It just makes sense that they should consult on these matters themselves first, rather than use precious Assembly meeting time. The External Affairs Office brings its recommendations to the whole Assembly where final consultation and decision-making take place.

Each of our External Affairs members is very articulate and we trust them when speaking with the media. If there isn't time to inform the Assembly at a meeting about an interview opportunity, the office will inform the rest of us by email of their decisions regarding an interview and which one of them will be doing it. That pre-approval is part of their office's mandate.

Other examples of offices in action:

- A Community Development Office might inform its Assembly that there is a need for education classes for new Bahá'ís, since there have been a number of recent enrolments. The office then presents an outline for such classes to the Assembly.

- A Teaching Office would update its Assembly on the work of the teaching committee, as well as some individual initiatives going on in the community.

Those kind of agenda items would have unnecessarily taken hours of Assembly time if the Assembly had had to discuss each detail from scratch. Offices or sub-committees can take action because the Assembly has mandated them to do so. *By appointing a few Assembly members to make certain decisions on behalf of the Assembly, those decisions become the Assembly's decisions.* When given a clearly written mandate from the Assembly, offices are able to act with maximum efficiency, all for the betterment of the Assembly.

Assembly offices or sub-committees are already being used by some local and national Bahá'í Assemblies. They have evolved as a useful tool for efficiency.

If your Assembly feels like it is always behind with its agenda, offices or sub-committees might be the answer. Between Assembly meetings the offices meet and move the work along. Since an office is only two or three people, its meetings are often held by phone, eliminating commuting time. Spending 45 minutes on the phone with your office colleagues is often more desirable than spending an entire evening out at yet another meeting. Could offices help *your* Assembly function more effectively?

Liaisons

Another means of 'getting things done' is to appoint Assembly liaisons to committees, tasks and events. Liaisons can exist instead of, or as well as, Assembly offices. A liaison is one Assembly member who is responsible for keeping the Assembly up to date on an item. Need an update on the Riḍván Festival plans? Ask the liaison. If the Riḍván Festival task force has questions about its mandate, they will call the liaison. The liaison is responsible for having the latest information available at the Assembly meetings. She also is the person who communicates back to the committees or task people with the Assembly's latest decisions and requests. Having liaisons keeps channels of communication functioning smoothly.

Telephone Conferencing

A telephone conference certainly reduces time spent commuting. Task forces and Assembly offices that use phone conferencing report that they are better at staying up-to-date on their projects, thanks to short and frequent phone conferences. Waiting until everyone can physically be at the same place at the same time delays meetings. Phone conferencing also spares some members from needing to arrange childcare.

The phone conference, however, is not ideal for all occasions. Philosophical or policy-making decisions are better left for in-person meetings. Phone conferencing skills are best practised in smaller offices and task forces before attempting them in nine-member Assemblies. Phone conferencing is effective when the items being consulted upon are very clear. 'How many travelling teachers do we want to see arise from our community this summer?' 'Are there any youth we should be sponsoring to attend the upcoming winter school?' These questions are specific and keep the participants focused. General consultation on the most recent Riḍván message from the Universal House of Justice, for example, would be more difficult by phone.

The following are tips for effective phone conferencing:

Have a good chairperson. The art of telephone chairing is different from in-person chairing. You cannot send or receive any visual cues!

Set a time limit for your meeting and stick to it.

Have the agenda known to all members in advance. Try to form the agenda with clear and specific questions.

Pause between speakers. Two people speaking at once is even more confusing on the phone. Wait for the chair to say your name.

Many Bahá'ís report that the occasional phone conference makes them better consultors in person. Acute and respectful listening skills are required and honed.

The satisfaction derived from a brief yet effective phone conference from home leaves the Bahá'í feeling good about maintaining a balance between Bahá'í service and spending quality time at home.

Email Decision-making

Some Assemblies make basic decisions by email. While this method cannot replace in-person consultation, it can save Assembly members from making eight phone calls when an urgent or simple matter arises.

Gwen explains:

This year our Assembly started using email for simple decision-making. We can't really call it 'email consultation' because we don't hear and respond to each other in the same spirit as when we are together in person but it really does help with routine items.

The method we use is this. One of us sends out a question to the other eight, such as 'The children's education committee is requesting $100 for a small filing cabinet. Do you approve?' If all eight respond with an unhesitating 'yes', then the committee would be told it can go ahead and buy the cabinet.

But one Assembly member might email back, 'The deepening committee is also in need of storage space. Perhaps a larger filing cabinet should be purchased and shared by several committees.' All email discussion on this matter would then stop and it would be tabled for proper consultation at a regularly scheduled in-person meeting.

All Assemblies from time to time find themselves with

the need to deal with a matter urgently. We have a policy that an urgent email must be responded to within 48 hours, preferably the same day. The person sending the original question polls the responses and takes the action. Because our Assembly approved this method after a careful in-person consultation, we feel the action person is acting with the Assembly's blessing.

Say the outgoing question is, 'A comparative religions class at the university has asked us to send a representative to address a class of 200 students for a 30-minute intro-duction to the Bahá'í Faith. The class is on Friday! This is an opportunity I feel we should grasp and I told them we would send someone. Brenda R. is available and willing. Do you approve?' Suppose six people write back saying 'yes', one says 'okay, but John M. would be better' and one person doesn't respond in time. This matter would be considered approved by a majority. The sender of the message would call Brenda to thank her and accept her offer on behalf of the Assembly.

This method of decision-making allows us to respond to issues in a timely fashion instead of always saying 'The Assembly meets next weekend. We'll get back to you.' But email decision-making only works if all nine members are committed to helping it work. If one member isn't on-line or is tardy in reading his emails, then the Assembly is denied his input.

Recording these email decisions is just as important as recording any made in person at meetings! We document 'Email Decisions' as an addendum in our next minutes.

Supporting Decisions

Consensus is the goal in consultation. Voting when

there is a difference of views is not to be rushed into just to make the meeting go faster. You'll not only miss out on the spark of truth that results from the clash of opinions but it also puts you at a higher risk of disharmony among members.

> The members thereof must take counsel together in such wise that no occasion for ill-feeling or discord may arise. This can be attained when every member expresseth with absolute freedom his own opinion and setteth forth his argument. Should anyone oppose, he must on no account feel hurt for not until matters are fully discussed can the right way be revealed. The shining spark of truth cometh forth only after the clash of differing opinions. If after discussion, a decision be carried unanimously well and good; but if, the Lord forbid, differences of opinion should arise, a majority of voices must prevail.[1]

Once your Assembly has made a decision, support it wholeheartedly! I would go beyond saying 'support it even if you voted otherwise' and say 'support it *especially* if you voted otherwise'. The spiritual institution has made its ruling. Disappointed? Get over it immediately and move on. Harbouring 'you'll see I'm right later' thoughts can impair an Assembly's functioning.

I was impressed during an Assembly meeting in which one member asked if he could be the task person for an item on which he strongly held the opposite view. It was his way of showing his obedience to, and support for, his Assembly. He carried the task through magnificently! He explained the Assembly's decision clearly to community members, knowing he was expressing the decision of the *institution* and not just the opinion of his

Assembly colleagues who held that view.

Sometimes Assemblies have to make difficult decisions. Some members of the community might voice their discontent in quite a challenging way. Assembly work is parenting work. Stand by your decisions. The visible unity of your Assembly will radiate throughout the community. When children see that their parents are united, they respect their parents and the family unit is stronger. Otherwise, children will try to play their parents off one another. Likewise, your Assembly unity has to be unwavering and evident to all.

Moving on with Decisions

Assemblies can be slowed down if they linger once a decision is made. If you follow the advice given in the above writings you can move on with your agenda. Bringing up the matter again, repeating why you disagree is of no benefit and wastes the Assembly's time. We are assured that where unity exists, God will make a wrong right.

> If they agree upon a subject, even though it be wrong, it is better than to disagree and be in the right, for this difference will produce the demolition of the divine foundation. Though one of the parties may be in the right and they disagree that will be the cause of a thousand wrongs, but if they agree and both parties are in the wrong, as it is in unity the truth will be revealed and the wrong made right.[2]

We all have a right to our opinions, we are bound to think differently; but a Bahá'í must accept the majority decision

of his Assembly, realizing that acceptance and harmony –
even if a mistake has been made – are the really important things, and when we serve the Cause properly, in the
Bahá'í way, God will right any wrongs done in the end.[3]

Policy Manuals

Assemblies are faced with the same questions again
and again by community members who don't know the
issue has previously been before the Assembly. When a
new member is elected onto an Assembly, she doesn't
know all of the earlier Assembly discussions and decisions, either. In the middle of a consultation it is often
heard, 'Didn't we have this same conversation last
year? What was our decision on it back then?' If
another person with a good memory was also on last
year's Assembly, then the decision might be remembered. Otherwise, the new Assembly will be holding

A policy manual is invaluable

the consultation from the beginning. The members might think to research the minutes. This is where a policy manual is *invaluable*.

When an Assembly makes a decision that it wants to be an ongoing policy, that item in the minutes can be copied and filed in a policy manual. If filed well, any standing policy can be easily found. Filing of policy decisions must be tasked to one person who keeps the manual up to date.

Policies are not over-administration. They enable an Assembly to function efficiently without re-inventing the wheel at each meeting. An example of a policy decision is: 'The Bahá'í Centre can be rented to non-Bahá'í groups and individuals for $30.00 an hour.' This spares the Assembly discussing how much to charge people each time a new request comes forward.

Of course, policies are not fixed for life. If new and valid reasons are presented in the months and years to come, an Assembly will change its policies to reflect the current state of affairs. Meanwhile, the manual enables the Assembly to move on with *new* matters requiring its consultation. Having a policy manual is a time management sensibility.

The Annual Report

To some, it is the dreaded annual report. It is that time-consuming thing in which an Assembly has to summarize its community's highlights (or low lights) over the past year. Even if such a document were not requested by the National Spiritual Assembly, performing an annual review would still be a valuable exercise for any Local Spiritual Assembly.

Preparing such a report causes an Assembly to take an honest inventory of its achievements. How close did we come to reaching the goals set for us by the Universal House of Justice, the National Assembly, our Bahá'í Council and ourselves? Did we exceed them? Were we even headed in the right direction? It doesn't matter how busy you were if you were going the wrong way.

To make the year-end job easier, an Assembly can assign one of its members the task of noting the items that are included in the annual report all year long (statistics, events, etc.). Do not assume this has to fall on the shoulders of the already busy secretary. Anyone can do it. Then when it comes time to prepare the final report it is simply a matter of organizing the already gathered data.

If your Assembly uses offices as discussed in the previous section, another method of preparing the annual report is to delegate various sections of the report to the appropriate offices. The sections can later be brought together in a completed and comprehensive annual report.

If neither of these approaches is used, well-written minutes are the answer. Obtaining the data for the report does require that somebody (or somebodies) go through all of the minutes from the past year's Assembly meetings and pick out the relevant information. Well-written minutes with highlighted decisions make this task so much easier.

Mid-term Review

An Assembly need not wait until the end of its term before reviewing its performance and the health of the community. At least once a year, and preferably more often, an Assembly can designate one of its meetings for an internal review. Some Assemblies do so while going on a one- or two-day retreat.

The following are five straightforward questions an Assembly can ask itself in a mid-term self-evaluation:

How is the Assembly's unity? Are all members free from estrangement?

What is our style of consultation? Are we striving to exhibit the prime requisites for consultation? ('The prime requisites for them that take counsel together are purity of motive, radiance of spirit, detachment from all else save God, attraction to His Divine Fragrances, humility and lowliness amongst His loved ones, patience and long-suffering in difficulties and servitude to His exalted Threshold.'[4])

How is the health and vitality of our community? Is our community an attraction to people who are not Bahá'ís?

Where are we with regard to the goals we have set for our community (teaching, deepening, percentage in fund participation and so on)?

Does the Assembly have a healthy and open relationship with the community?

Taking such an inventory mid-year or quarterly enables an Assembly to adjust its rudder as needed.

Keeping Project Notes

It is highly advisable that you make notes right after holding an event you helped plan. Let's say you and a few friends organized a magnificent 12th Day of Riḍván celebration. By keeping your planning notes in a file you greatly reduce the amount of work required next time an event like this is planned. When something wonderful takes place, people think they will never forget the details but if they don't write them down, they generally *do* forget.

> 'The food was so delicious, I'll never forget that caterer!'
> 'We got such a good deal on the flowers, I'll never forget where we bought them.'
> 'The band had such a cute name, I'll never forget who they are.'
> 'The table cloths fit so well, I'll never forget what size to use next time.'

The above statements and many more like them have been said over and over by Bahá'ís, all of whom forgot precisely what they swore they could never possibly forget. In the heat of a happy moment we think the information is imprinted on us forever but without hypnosis we all have trouble retrieving ageing information.

After an event, immediately make a written evaluation of what went well and what could have been better.

> 'The acoustics at the community hall on 12th avenue are poor and I don't recommend renting it again.'

'Pianist Mrs Smith is excellent! Her phone number is
222–2222.'

'We planned four hors d'oeuvres per person; not
enough. Recommend six.'

'Very appropriate scriptures were read. Copies kept
in file.'

The merit in making notes after an event is that it benefits the *event*, whether or not you are involved with it
next time. People move or serve on new committees.
But if the information is retained and filed, whoever is
planning it next time will be grateful and will continue
to improve on the event.

Assemblies can consider requiring such notes, even if
very brief, from the people it delegates to look after
projects. A file kept by the Assembly makes for easier
research next time.

14

Time Management for New Bahá'ís

Time for the Faith

'There are two kinds of people in the world . . . those who put people into two categories and those who don't.' Joking aside, there are two kinds of Bahá'ís . . . those who are born into Bahá'í families and those who aren't.

There can be big differences in how these two types of Bahá'ís assimilate the Faith into their lives. Growing up in a Bahá'í household, a child sees people fasting, saying obligatory prayers, going to Feast, pioneering and so on. These are common aspects of Bahá'í life. The child grows up surrounded by these behaviours and considers them normal.

To become a Bahá'í later in life can be a big change for an individual. It is a welcome and willing change but nonetheless it introduces several new behaviours into one's life that weren't there before. Some of these new practices have implications on the new Bahá'í's time and how he manages it.

'I've always been an active person,' says Mary, a Bahá'í for a year and a half. 'I work part-time, I used to volunteer regularly at my community league, I used to take yoga lessons. Now I help at Bahá'í school every weekend and try to attend as many deepenings as I can. I attend Nineteen Day Feasts and Holy Days and go to talks by special speakers. The other day I sat down and had a good look at my life. I had to ask myself: Whatever happened to serving at my community league and yoga lessons? I don't seem to go any more. And what about my friends who aren't Bahá'ís? I hardly ever see them. I'm always with my new Bahá'í friends or attending one Bahá'í function or another. How did this happen to my life? I used to think I was a busy person before but now I'm even busier. I look back and now I miss what seems to be the simplicity of my life before I was a Bahá'í.'

Mary is overwhelmed by the changes in her life since becoming a Bahá'í but this does not have to happen. If you were not born into a Bahá'í family and embraced this Faith through your own discovery, be practical and patient with the pace at which you become involved in the Bahá'í community. The Bahá'í Faith is God's gift to your soul. It is not here to throw your personal life into

I'VE BEEN ASKED TO HOST THIS FEAST BY THE WAY ..... WHAT IS A FEAST ?!?

disarray and cause you resentment because you are too busy.

Sometimes Bahá'ís will get excited when someone newly declares and they are eager to welcome and involve the newcomer in community life. If this is done without being sensitive to the individual's personal situation, however, some overtures can be inappropriate and overwhelm the new Bahá'í. I have seen overly stressed Bahá'ís pounce on newcomers to join their projects because they themselves have become too busy. They see the new person as another available pair of hands to help with the work. Sensitivity to what is best for the new Bahá'í should be foremost.

Since all Bahá'ís are at their own stages of development, there will be various expressions of awareness of how to best welcome newcomers. If you are a new Bahá'í and you feel you are receiving too many invitations to become involved in Bahá'í community life in a short period of time, say so. Be selective and do not feel you have to attend everything. You are right to choose your own priorities.

Knowing which Bahá'í practices are laws and which are not is helpful. Prayer and fasting are laws, for example, and both require a little time management. Attending celebrations and going to meetings are not obligatory however. While attending Holy Day events is spiritually enriching, if one day you feel tired and haven't seen enough of your family lately, stay home with them instead of going to the Bahá'í function. You are not expected to attend every Bahá'í event there is.

Emily is a wife and mother of three school-age children. She and her family became Bahá'ís four years ago.

'There are so many things to learn when you become a Bahá'í!' she said. 'There are new Holy Days to observe, Nineteen Day Feasts, Ayyám-i-Há and so on. Because the calendar day actually begins the evening before, I'm usually confused as to when to show up for Feast!

'The first year was a bit overwhelming, but now I've learned to pace myself. I don't try to go to everything any more. With each passing year, I seem to embrace a new Holy Day and understand it better. Last year I really got into the Festival of Riḍván. I participated in every event and really absorbed the significance of the festival. This year it was the Ascension of Bahá'u'lláh. Our whole family stayed up late and went to the com-memoration. We stayed home from work and school the next day. Now I have a much better appreciation for that particular Holy Day. Each year I seem to be adding one or two more Holy Days to my repertoire of understanding. I think integrating Bahá'í events should be a gradual thing, otherwise you can burn yourself out in the first year.'

She also describes how Ayyám-i-Há becomes more significant to her family each year. 'This year Ayyám-i-Há really felt special to us. We gave our children gifts each day of Ayyám-i-Há. We went to a couple of par-ties as a family. We spent one afternoon having a family play-day at an indoor swimming pool. It was the most festive Ayyám-i-Há we've had yet.

'The kids seem to be making the transition to Bahá'í life better than my husband and I, perhaps because we joined the Faith while they were young. Last Christmas we gave each child a new comic book and a bag of candy. They were thrilled because they weren't expecting anything! Ayyám-i-Há is their holiday now.'

Kate describes how she tried phasing out her Christmas celebrations, which had been important to her all her life before joining the Bahá'í Faith.

'For the first five years of being a Bahá'í I didn't celebrate Christmas at all. Since I was married to a Bahá'í and all my relatives live several hours away, not having a Christmas tree seemed easy for me to live with. Then this year it really bothered me. Christmas had always been a *family* occasion for me, not a religious one. Why was I giving up the family ties and traditions that meant so much to me? I was trying too hard to adopt the Bahá'í holidays and pretend the old ones didn't matter to me any more, but they did.

'So this year I bought a tiny artificial tree and set it up on a table in a corner of our living room. I still receive Christmas gifts from my sisters and parents, who are not Bahá'ís, so I put them under my little tree. Looking at that tree made me feel close to my family and brought back so many happy childhood memories. I do put a greater effort into celebrating Ayyám-i-Há but this year I had to be honest with myself and acknowledge that I wasn't ready yet to entirely give up the family side of Christmas.'

When to start participating in the Bahá'í community is individually timed. You do not need to feel thrown into the deep end of the pool as the above people did. Some people are attracted to the social network of the Bahá'í community and instantly want to be part of it. Participating in a community service project alongside new Bahá'í friends is just what they need. Some new Bahá'ís are so enthused by Bahá'u'lláh's Revelation that they rush to share the news with others, immediately joining a teaching project. Others take their time before attending Bahá'í functions and joining service opportunities. One way to participate in community life that also builds your confidence as a Bahá'í and gradually introduces you to other paths of service is the training institute's study circle. Trust your intuition and do what inherently feels right for you. The Bahá'í community will always be there, with open arms and loving hearts to welcome you when you are ready.

As one new Bahá'í expressed, 'I kept saying "no" when people asked me to help with Bahá'í things. Could I prepare the readings for this, bring a dessert for that. I was really busy – but busy doing what? Serving *my* interests or *Bahá'u'lláh's*? One day the short obligatory prayer hit me like lightning. "Thou hast created me to know Thee and to worship Thee." That's my purpose! To know and worship God! Nothing more, nothing less. I then realized that much of my daily running around was in service to *me*. Once I took on a more active role in the Bahá'í community I began to feel better about myself and my reason for being alive.'

Time for Prayer

This book advocates writing a daily list of the things one wants to do. For a new Bahá'í, daily prayer and meditation might be on that list while these are still new practices. It is necessary to remind oneself to pray until praying becomes a habit, like brushing one's teeth. Brushing your teeth is likely not on your 'To Do' list, since you automatically do it every day. But flossing your teeth might be written down if you've made a recent resolution to floss daily. Many Bahá'ís pray at the same time each day and it does become a habit not easily forgotten.

A Bahá'í who joined the Faith just over a year ago recounted the following story:

A man who had grown up in a Bahá'í family scoffed in front of me once at how ridiculous an idea it could be for a Bahá'í to need to write down a reminder to say his daily obligatory prayer. 'How could someone possibly miss *that?*' he ridiculed. 'I do,' I thought, but I didn't tell him so. He went on to say that for him, saying the long obligatory prayer before going to bed was the most beautiful time of his day. He had memorized it as a youth and couldn't imagine a day without doing it. He seemed unaware that for many new Bahá'ís prayer of any kind could be a totally new experience.

This Bahá'í and I also disagreed on which prayer was 'best' to say. Again he scoffed at the idea of someone only saying the short obligatory prayer. I asked him for a reference from the writings that says it is better to say the long obligatory prayer. He was silent for a moment because we both knew there isn't one. Instead, he offered his own rationale: 'When you say the long obligatory prayer you get swept away in its beauty. Its long enough for it to be a spiritual experience.'

I try the long obligatory prayer sometimes but I have to admit, I catch myself having thoughts like 'What page am I on? Am I half way through yet?' so I asked him, 'Isn't it better for someone to pray sincerely for 20 seconds than insincerely for 11 minutes?' He shrugged, no doubt wondering why people just don't get sincere with the long obligatory prayer.

My goal is still to memorize the medium and long

obligatory prayers. I find it awkward to read from a prayer book while my forehead is down on the carpet. I suppose those are the parts to memorize first. Until then, I like saying the short obligatory prayer. I do it with sincerity, even joy, and I'm obeying God.

I admire this new Bahá'í for not being intimidated by the older, opinionated Bahá'í. I'm sure his sentiments are shared by many new Bahá'ís.

The Fast

It is often difficult for us to do things because they are so very different from what we are used to, not because the thing itself is particularly difficult. With you, and indeed most Bahá'ís, who are now, as adults, accepting this glorious Faith, no doubt some of the ordinances, like fasting and daily prayer, are hard to understand and obey at first. But we must always think that these things are given to all men for a thousand years to come. For Bahá'í children who see these things practised in the home, they will be as natural and necessary a thing as going to church on Sunday was to the more pious generation of Christians. Bahá'u'lláh would not have given us these things if they would not greatly benefit us, and, like children who are sensible enough to realize their father is wise and does what is good for them, we must accept to obey these ordinances even though at first we may not see any need for them. As we obey them we will gradually come to see in ourselves the benefits they confer.[1]

Nothing impacts a new Bahá'í's time quite like the fast

does. You find yourself rising to pray and eat before sunrise, then waiting until after sunset to eat and drink again. None of these practices you did before. It is impossible not to notice the fast. This cycle goes on for 19 consecutive days during the month of 'Alá each and every year.

If we lived in a time and place where sleep cycles naturally mirrored the sun's comings and goings, fasting would blend in with reasonable ease. There would be a slight adjustment in dining times but no real stress about it. However, we are now living in a 24-hour society. We are a culture of busy people rushing about, trying to get things done, and now we're fasting too.

You will note that the Bahá'í writings do not provide fasting exemptions for people who are time-challenged. You don't get to eat a half hour earlier than the rest of us because you have evening meetings to get to. Nor do shift workers get to adjust the fasting times to better suit their schedules. (As a shift worker myself, I am sympathetic.) The sun rises and sets when it does, irrespective of your work schedule and the Bahá'í laws of fasting are attached to those rhythms of the sun. This does pose a major challenge to some people, such as shift workers. The inflexibility of the laws does not mean God is unsympathetic and unloving. If adhering to fasting times is a test for you, then bless your test. Envying people who do not have your challenging work schedule would be fruitless.

Glen works in a factory which has three shifts: day, evening and night. Low in seniority, Glen has a schedule in which he rotates all three shifts. He describes the effects his shift work has on fasting:

When I work days, I'm up at 6:00. During the fast I get up at 5:30 so I have more time for prayer and a good breakfast. That's not hard.

On night shift I sleep most of the day. I have supper with my wife in the evening and then I nibble a lot through the night. It's just like any normal night shift. I don't even feel like I'm fasting. I've felt guilty about it and wondered if I should switch to fasting during the night while I'm up instead. I read all I could about it and consulted with friends but nothing in the writings supports doing that. Just because I don't feel food-deprived on nights doesn't mean I'm not fasting. I am. I'm obeying the law of fasting. I pray more and I'm conscious of the fast. I just happen to sleep through the day.

It's on evening shift that the fast is a challenge for me. Off at midnight, I'm home just before 1:00. I unwind for a bit and go to bed around 2:00. Normally I sleep until 9:00 or 10:00 a.m. That means sunrise is right in the middle of my sleep. I've tried everything. Eating a meal right before bed doesn't agree with my stomach and it keeps me awake. Sometimes I sleep through sunrise and don't eat until sunset but that leaves me feeling weak at the start of my shift at 4:00. When I get up before sunrise (in the middle of my 'night') to pray and eat with my wife I'm so groggy I often eat quickly and fall asleep again without any real spiritual focus. I don't know what to do. I don't have a system figured out yet for evening shift. I keep telling myself the fast isn't about when I eat, its my obedience to a spiritual law. I just have to figure out what to do on these evening shifts.

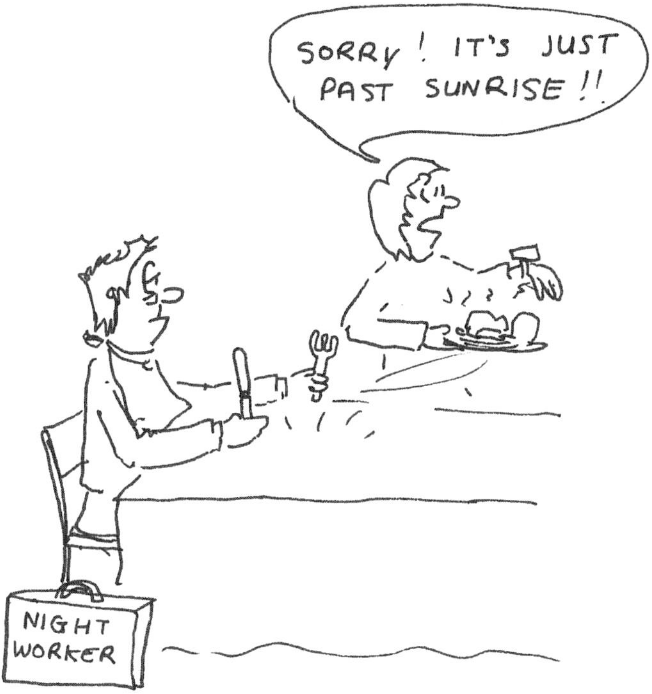
SORRY! IT'S JUST PAST SUNRISE!!
NIGHT WORKER

Glen is not alone. There are many shift workers and people with other circumstances that make the timing of fasting interesting for them. And he's absolutely right: The fast is not about when to eat and not eat. By focusing on the spiritual benefits you reap through your obedience to the fast, your logistical troubles seem smaller.

The fast serves a spiritual purpose. It is a physically outward action serving an inward spiritual purpose. Whether or not we are aware of any spiritual transformation within us, it is taking place.

> The fasting period, which lasts nineteen days starting as a rule from the second of March every year and ending on the twentieth of the same month, involves complete abstention from food and drink from sunrise till sunset. It is essentially a period of meditation and prayer, of spiritual recuperation, during which the believer must strive to make the necessary readjustments in his inner life, and to refresh and reinvigorate the spiritual forces latent in his soul. Its significance and purpose are, therefore, fundamentally spiritual in character. Fasting is symbolic, and a reminder of abstinence from selfish and carnal desires.[2]

Fasting Strategies

While keeping the spiritual benefits of the fast in mind, if you still feel time-challenged by the fast, consider the following:

Know that there are many Bahá'ís like you. Some have circumstances identical to yours, such as the time constraints of work and family life. They too are fasting along with you.

Do not feel that you must eat immediately at sunset. If you feel too rushed to have supper at sunset, have some water and a snack. Then later, when you have time to sit and enjoy a meal without hurrying, have your supper.

Bask in the many teaching opportunities the fast affords you. When you explain to colleagues and others you meet why you are not eating or drinking with them, you have conversations about the Faith that would not otherwise occur.

Read and pray more. It can be a marvellous period of both spiritual and physical rejuvenation. Most Bahá'ís say they love the fast for the strengthening of their spiritual connection to Bahá'u'lláh. They read more, pray more, meditate more. They promise to keep up this level of reading and praying and meditating after the fast. Some even do it. Others get reminded of its wonders again during the next fast.

But too few Bahá'ís claim to feel physically refreshed after the fast. Many say they are exhausted. They maintained all their usual activities but on less sleep. They went to bed at their usual times but got up earlier.

Get more sleep. If your usual bedtime is midnight, during the next fast make a pledge to go to bed at 10:30 every night. 'But I won't be tired,' you say. Good. Go to bed anyway. Read a book. Be with your spouse. Rest.

You will start falling asleep earlier. You will wake up refreshed. Your whole day will be illumined with serenity rather than overshadowed by fatigue.

Simply do less. It's only 19 days, for goodness sake. Your body won't atrophy if you don't go to the gym. The groups you belong to won't stop existing if you don't attend a couple of meetings. Go home and rest. Spend time with your loved ones. Don't answer the phone every time it rings. Look at your fast through the eyes of your children. Are you setting an example of hurry and fatigue or are you an example of fasting that your children look forward to copying?

Imagine the majority of people in your city or country following the Bahá'í fast. Business and school hours might be adjusted for the month. Afternoon naps could be the norm. Everyone would be fasting. You would feel supported in your fast and in harmony with all around you. Wouldn't that be a beautiful environment to live in? Perhaps someday our descendants will have such a life. For now, however, you and I are living in our current circumstances. Think of our fast as the cornerstone on which the months of 'Alá of the future will be built.

Requests vs. Appointments

Being called into service is something that will eventually happen to a new Bahá'í, therefore it warrants being mentioned here. Bahá'í service is generated through four means – individual initiative, requests, appointments and elections.

Individual initiative is any idea you have on your own which you offer up to your community. Offering to play guitar at a Nineteen Day Feast is an individual initiative. If the Feast committee comes to you first and asks you to perform, this is a request and you will say yes or no. Those two doors of service are straightforward and the Bahá'í chooses his level of involvement.

Appointments and elections, however, are different. If the Assembly *appoints* you to serve on the Feast committee, it is not a request. The appointment means you are now on that committee. 'Can I give you my decision later?' is not an appropriate answer. 'Thank you. I will do my best to serve' is better. This is how Bahá'í administration works.

Imagine if a community elected an Assembly and after the election all nine Assembly members said, 'No thanks. I'm too busy. I've got a job and a family, you know. I can't possibly serve on the Assembly.' Bahá'í administration wouldn't function. Being elected to an Assembly means you are now on the Assembly.

This does not mean there is never an exit from an appointed or elected position. The Faith is far too practical and loving for such insensitivity to occur. Sometimes an individual's personal circumstances do permit him to resign. If you ever find yourself in a position of needing to be relieved of service, just let the appropriate institution of the Faith know and all the loving assistance you require will be showered upon you.

One way to prevent being appointed to a committee that does not appeal to you is to let your Assembly know where your interests do lie. If teaching music to children is your passion, then your Assembly can strive to give you an appointment where this talent will shine.

Mature Assemblies are sensitive to the individual conditions of newer Bahá'ís. They will offer opportunities for service without taxing newcomers unwisely.

No Room for Boredom

'I'm bored.' Honestly, I haven't heard a Bahá'í say that. I've heard lots of people say they are bored but not my Bahá'í friends. 'On the weekend I clean my house and then what? I get bored,' I heard a work colleague say. Oh, to have such troubles, I thought.

Once a person recognizes the call of Bahá'u'lláh within his heart, things change forever. The Bahá'í will never have 'nothing to do'. There is self improvement and the work of the Cause, both of which will last throughout the Bahá'í's lifetime. Upon becoming a Bahá'í, however, boredom should not be replaced with stress and exhaustion. Yes, the work of the Cause must be done but you don't have to complete it all by yourself before Tuesday afternoon. Pace yourself. Determine the kind of Bahá'í you aspire to be and make your plan.

When Your Spouse is not a Bahá'í

Becoming the first Bahá'í in your family is breaking new ground. You are a pioneer. This is a monumental decision you have made which could change the course of your life. If you are married and your spouse has not shared your investigation of the Bahá'í Faith, your new habits could puzzle him. Suddenly you are going to Nineteen Day Feasts ('Is that all you Bahá'ís do? Eat?'), Holy Day commemorations, study circles, deepenings and, strangest of all, you fast for 19 days!

If you have your spouse's support and encouragement, despite his not wanting to become a Bahá'í, I applaud your marriage. Giving each other room to learn and grow is a sign of a healthy marriage. However, if your spouse remains uncertain about your Bahá'í life, take things slowly. Now is not the time to run off on a two month travel teaching trip with your new Bahá'í friends.

Assure your spouse of your love for him. Your new Faith and new friends have not arrived to take you away from him. Share with him some writings that expound the importance of the family and a committed marriage. Tell him of the ways you believe the Bahá'í Faith will make you a better person, the virtues you aspire to embody and how this will make you a better marriage partner.

> The relationship between husband and wife must be viewed in the context of the Bahá'í ideal of family life. Bahá'u'lláh came to bring unity to the world, and a fundamental unity is that of the family. Therefore, one must believe that the Faith is intended to strengthen the family, not weaken it . . .[3]

If you are ever torn between your family and your Bahá'í activities, choose your family. Without united families at its foundation, the Bahá'í community falters. We cannot establish a united Bahá'í community and united world until we first practise unity at home.

> In considering the problems that you and your wife are experiencing, the House of Justice points out that the

unity of your family should take priority over any other consideration . . . For example, service to the Cause should not produce neglect of the family. It is important for you to arrange your time so that your family life is harmonious and your household receives the attention it requires.[4]

Becoming a Bahá'í should be a beautiful addition to your life. If it is presented to your spouse in the right fashion, he will see that when you do something this beneficial for yourself it is good for the whole family.

15

Short Subjects

The following is a series of perspectives that relate to time and life management in various ways. None of these sections is big enough to warrant its own chapter, therefore they appear here together in one eclectic buffet of food for thought.

Blame

Why would there be a section on blame in a time and life management book? Because many people do blame others for the circumstances they are experiencing in their own lives.

'My parents over-fed me as a child and I'm still fat.'

'My parents were poor and could not afford to send me to college. That's why I have a low-paying job.'

'My sister is prettier. That's why I never have a date.'

'The government isn't doing enough for job creation. That's why I'm unemployed.'

'My wife is lazy. If she'd exercise with me, I'd be more fit.'

You might think you're not a blamer but it doesn't hurt to do a personal inventory anyway. Dig deep. Is there any circumstance in your life for which you point the causative finger at someone or something outside yourself? If you started smoking at the age of 16 because you were hanging around with the wrong kids, look around you now. Those old friends are gone. It's time to take ownership of your addiction and stop blaming the kid who gave you that first cigarette. If everyone in your family is clumsy and you want to learn to ballroom dance, then be the first one in your lineage to train himself to be graceful.

If you pause for a moment and spot a predicament or two in your life for which you blame the economy, your boss, your spouse, anything or anyone other than yourself for the condition you are in, release the object of your blame immediately. Granted, circumstances that seem beyond our control appear to shape our lives but our *responses* to these circumstances are within our sole command.

Once a person takes responsibility for his reactions, a remarkable feeling of empowerment accompanies that acknowledgement. This empowerment gives the individual the creativity and stamina necessary to enact change. That weight off your shoulders will make you feel inches taller. The breath you inhale will be more invigorating. Your surroundings will come alive with opportunity.

It behoveth you, therefore, to attach blame to no one except to yourselves, for the things ye have committed, if ye but judge fairly.[1]

If you are waiting for circumstances to change before you get better organized, then you could be waiting for a very long time. You will also probably be disappointed to discover that you don't change even when the circumstances do. 'If I had a new purse I would keep it tidy all the time.' Yeah, sure. Get your present handbag organized and show yourself you are worthy of a new one. Otherwise we both know the new handbag will be a cluttered mess in no time. Wherever you go, there you are. You cannot run away from your habits. You have to improve them wherever you are. Moving to a better house, to a different Bahá'í community, to a different job is not going to change *your* behaviour. Face yourself head-on wherever you are and start implementing new strategies for living now. There is a saying, 'Blame your parents for how you turned out, if you like. But only blame yourself if you stay that way.'

> People are always blaming their circumstances for what they are.
> I don't believe in circumstances.
> The people who get on in this world are the people who get up
> and look for the circumstances they want, and,
> if they can't find them, make them.
> *George Bernard Shaw*

Diaries

Have you ever kept a diary, perhaps in your youth or childhood? Many people have, if only for a trial period. It is a therapeutic means of sorting out one's thoughts and feelings. It is also nostalgic when reminiscing years later. Very few adults, though, can say they have mastered the art of keeping a daily journal.

Nightly reflection on 'What kind of person was I today?' is valuable for a Bahá'í who's checking if his behaviours that day were in line with his governing values and 'To Be' list. 'Was I polite and patient with others? Did I mention the name Bahá'u'lláh to at least one new person today?' Reviewing in one's mind what kind of person one was each day is beneficial.

Writing a diary is too precious an art to be forgotten because we 'don't have time'. Yet making daily diary entries is an unrealistic priority for most of us. I have an effective alternative I wish to share with you. It's called the annual diary.

It's just as it sounds. You write in a diary once a year. I use 1 January but Naw-Rúz, your birthday or any other special day would also work well. You will likely need an hour of uninterrupted contemplative time. I get up on 1 January and make a cup of tea. Hopefully there is snow falling outside, which I can enjoy watching through the window. Taking the tea and a notebook back to bed with me, I write my diary for the year. It takes one to two pages usually. The entries are normally brief, with a few elaborations. For example:

Highlights of (year):

Attended Grandma's 80th birthday party in Hamilton. It was great to see relatives I haven't seen for years.

My sister Laura had her first baby! I'm an auntie again!

Took a night course in public speaking.

Volunteered at the Street Performer's Festival.

Three of my regular fireside guests (Anne, Barry and Joseph) became Bahá'ís this year.

Took a three-week vacation in September to the Maritimes. It was so beautiful! I'd love to go again.

I sprained my foot when a horse stepped on it at riding lessons.

Attended the *Fundamental Verities* deepening series at the Bahá'í Centre.

I read *The Priceless Pearl*. Reading about the sacrifices the Guardian made quite an impact on me.

Attended Donna's funeral. Our friendship became very close in her last few weeks.

This is a partial list but I think you get the idea. Try to include a statement from all major areas of your life (spiritual, emotional, physical, mental). Listing a favourite movie you saw or book you read will make you smile when you read your diary in years to come. These are the little details that are easily forgotten yet symbolize what was important to you for a while. Mention the friends who were most dear to you. Comment on your 'To Be' list and how on-track this year was.

Unless you are a famous person whose memoirs will

really matter one day, a day-by-day accounting of your thoughts and actions will likely never be read by anyone, even you. If you do ever read your old daily diaries, you will only skim them, lingering over a few pages. An annual diary, however, is fun to reread. Before I make my new entries each January, I look over some of the past years.

If ever you think you haven't accomplished much or that the years are blurring into one another, your annual diary could amaze you. Every year I marvel at past and present achievements. I'm always making remarks such as, 'Wow! Did all that happen last year? That's quite a lot!' Looking back at previous years I am amused by what was important to me back then that is not in my life at all now. I reminisce about happy times spent with friends who may or may not still be nearby.

Experiment with writing an annual diary. You could start it right now. You might well be impressed with all that has happened in the past year of your life.

Reading

Books are the treasured wealth of the world
and the fit inheritance of generations and nations.
Their authors are a natural and irresistible aristocracy in
every society,
and more than kings or emperors, exert an influence on
mankind.
Henry David Thoreau

In the year 2000 the Arts and Entertainment television network on its programme *Biography* undertook the formidable task of naming the 100 most influential people of the millennium. So many impressive people have come and gone over the past 1000 years! Choosing the top 100 is difficult; selecting one person to hold the top position of Most Important Person of the Millennium is harder still. They wisely selected Johann Gutenberg (c.1400–68), the inventor of the printing press.

Prior to Gutenberg's invention, the books that did exist were handwritten with quill and ink. The few people who could read (usually those with religious or political power) dispensed information orally to the masses. This was a marvellously effective method for controlling people.

If you control what people know, you control the people.

With the advent of the printing press, the written word became available to everyone. Common people learned to read. Hence, the emancipation of the masses took place. People were learning, debating and thinking for themselves. Within 50 years of the introduction of the printing press, 20 million books had been printed in Europe alone.

> He must study every day from morning till noon, so that he may learn how to read and write. From noon till about sunset he should acquire a craft. The children must both learn to read and acquire an art or skill.[2]

Do you read every day? Bahá'ís are encouraged to read from the writings every morning and evening. That could mean spending a minute contemplating a brief passage in *The Hidden Words* or spending an hour reading from *Gleanings*. In the world of flying, a non-directional beacon (NDB) is a beacon that continually transmits navigational information. A pilot whose receiver is on can stay on course thanks to the NDBs. The Bahá'í writings serve as a spiritual NDB for anyone who chooses to read them.

Countless fascinating books have been written about the Bahá'í Faith and more are published every year. We have Bahá'í history, intriguing biographies of the heroes and heroines of the Cause, books about teaching and living the life. These books educate and consecrate the friends in the Faith. While it is tempting to have Bahá'í literature consume all of our reading time, it is advisable for Bahá'ís to be well-rounded with their reading materials. Bahá'ís need to be acutely aware of the times in which they live, including current published works, in order to effectively relate the teachings of Bahá'u'lláh to modern times.

The Guardian was an avid reader. In his youth he read extensively on a wide variety of subjects. Once appointed Guardian, he was particularly concerned with staying abreast of current world events. And he did all this while having the weight of the Bahá'í world on his shoulders. Amidst translating the writings, administering the affairs of the global Bahá'í community, while under attack from the Covenant-breakers, Shoghi Effendi made time to read two to three hours every day.[3]

Making Time to Read

The man who does not read good books
has no advantage over the man who can't read them.
Mark Twain

How do you make time to read if you feel your time is

already stretched beyond bearable limits? Look for little time pockets that lay hidden all around you. If you lower your expectations of how much should be read per session, you could be surprised by how much reading can be done over time. You can read one page while doing many other things – riding the subway, taking a bath, waiting for the kettle to boil.

I wanted to learn how the Guardian utilized his time, as part of the research for this book. I read *The Priceless Pearl* over numerous coffee breaks at work until eventually I had read it all. To say 'I want to read 451 pages to research one segment of my book' seems overwhelming but not if my expectation was to only read three pages per coffee break. In fact, I have been able to read many books a year using this strategy. Instead of sleeping or watching TV during my lunchtime at work, I read. Gradually this not only amounts to numerous books being read but also results in me completing a significant amount of research. I've seen people complete university courses using this gentle yet methodical approach.

When you are sitting in the bleachers at your son's football game, you could have a book open in your lap. Once in a while look down and read one paragraph. Before the play-off season starts you will have read a couple books *and* supported your son at his games.

Do you and your spouse or kids drive together to work or school in the mornings? Have one of them read a page aloud in the car while you drive. You will all have read the same book together and united yourselves in this shared family activity. Listening to books on cassette or CD is an excellent way to 'read' in the car.

To discover where new pockets of time exist in your life, try the following: For two or three days carry a book around with you all day, whenever appropriate. Because the book is physically present, it will frequently remind you to read. You will find yourself reading in moments previously unrecognized as potential reading breaks.

If you are a regular TV watcher, do you ever have an opportunity to amaze yourself with new time to read! Some people say, 'I don't really watch TV. It's only on when I'm having breakfast' or 'I just watch a little before going to sleep.' If these people experimented for one week and read during these times instead, a shocking amount of reading would be accomplished. Could you challenge yourself to a little less TV this week and a little more reading?

When you are reading a resource book, underline or highlight the parts you'd like to remember. Yes, I'm actually suggesting you mark up your good copy of *God Passes By* and everything else you read. Someday you will be preparing a talk for a Bahá'í function and want to find a passage you read once upon a time. Will you ever be grateful to find it highlighted and jumping off the page at you. Underlining makes the second reading of any book much faster, as it should be.

> We should not teach great books;
> we should teach a love of reading.
> *B. F. Skinner*

Slavery to Possessions

> Before we set our hearts too much on anything,
> let us examine how happy are those who already possess it.
> *La Rochefoucauld*

Our western culture is obsessed with owning things. For many people, if they like something, they must have it. This baffles me. Ownership can be such a burden. So much so it takes the pleasure right out of enjoying the very thing you wanted. What's so wrong with renting, borrowing or just admiring pretty things from a distance? My motto: Just because I like elephants doesn't mean I need to own one!

Rico and Janice have a cabin at the lake. They spend a few weeks there every summer but never as many as they say they will. Their careers and other responsibilities keep them busy. Every spring they prepare the cabin for summer. There is interior cleaning, exterior maintenance and copious yard work. Tired of mowing their large lot, Rico bought a riding mower last year. He then bought a shed in which to keep the mower and other equipment. Since their cabin is at a lake, they bought a boat. They take it out on the water whenever they are entertaining guests but seldom when it's just the two of them. Of course they have a trailer for hauling the boat back to the city at the end of the season. Their leisure time spent at the lake is overshadowed by the maintenance the cabin requires. If they aren't repairing steps, they are trying to remove a wasps' nest from under the eaves. If they aren't weeding the garden, they are repairing the motor on the boat.

Rico and Janice finally admitted to themselves that going to the lake wasn't fun anymore. Rather than anticipating relaxing on their deck, they were dreading the work their retreat would demand. Rico and Janice were slaves to their cabin.

They sat down together and listed on paper why they bought their cabin in the first place. They loved getting

away from the city and being amidst nature. They liked going for walks in the afternoon and barbecuing in the evening. They liked just being together, playing cards or doing a crossword puzzle on the deck – things they never seemed to make enough time for when they were at home in the city.

Then they listed what they didn't like about their cabin. It had only one extra bedroom for visitors. Their waterfront was rocky and not well-suited for swimming. The nearest restaurant was 45 minutes away and they did want to eat out once in a while. There was definitely more yard work and maintenance than they ever imagined. They also passed up opportunities for other summer vacations because they felt obliged to go to their cabin. After all, they had paid for it.

Rico and Janice realized they liked going to *a* cabin at the lake but not necessarily *this* cabin every year. Their decision to buy was influenced by the fact that several of their friends owned cabins. They didn't recognize when they made their purchase that they would have been happier as renters, not owners.

By renting a cabin instead they could have stayed at different lakes, enabling them to see more of their province. There would have been no arduous labour in setting up and closing the cabin; they could just turn in the keys when their holiday was over. If they wanted a different vacation one year instead, there would be no guilt about not using their cabin.

Rico and Janice sold their cabin. Having experienced the burden of ownership, they have a new appreciation of living a simpler life. Their vacations are relaxing again. They still accept invitations to visit friends who own cabins. They have found ways to enjoy the benefits of cottage life without the burden of ownership.

> He who multiplies riches, multiplies cares.
> *Ben Franklin*

Voluntary Simplicity

'Affluenza' is a disease of modern society. Its grip is fierce and competitive. Its victims are never satisfied and they never believe they finally have enough. The antidote for those who want to break free from this crippling disease is *voluntary simplicity*. The ability to say 'enough is enough and this is enough' is key to successfully managing both your time and your material space. Keeping your life uncomplicated is the surest way to sleep well at night.

There is an erroneous belief in our society that if you want to use something you should own it. Owning too many things has caused too many people too many headaches. I love horses, for example, and love to go riding a few times a year. There are moments when I'm riding that feel so joyous I think I ought to have my own horse. But horses require frequent grooming and riding, not to mention the cost of the horse itself plus monthly stable fees. (Or why not buy an acreage and have my own stable!) One has to be really passionate about horses to go to all that trouble and I'm not. My passion for horses lasts a few hours every year. Fortunately, I have a keen eye for recognizing how to experience passion but not be swept away and 'buy the whole farm' as they say. I am cautious about bringing anything into my life that requires a significant time commitment. Any new interest that requires a sizeable amount of time will by necessity take time away from another important interest in my life. If 'I want to be a horse owner' isn't high on my 'To Be' list, I should think twice before making an impulsive horse purchase.

People frequently make passionate purchases of big items like sailboats or large houses without honestly looking at the *time* price tag that comes attached. If you own stuff, it requires maintenance. And your time spent maintaining your purchases is probably time taken away from attending to the person you want to be. Even owning too much small stuff, like a houseful of decorative items that always need dusting, requires maintenance time. If you can learn to recognize when enough is enough, when it is better for you to rent or borrow something, when you can admire something without owning it (sport cars and horses included) you will then own peace of mind. And peace of mind has a much higher value than 'things'.

The truth is, we never really own anything. Even if we exchange our hard-earned cash for something, we don't keep it forever. When we move on to the next world all our material goods stay behind here on earth and somebody else starts using them. We are not the owners of things. We are merely stewards for a time. To appreciate things but not be consumed by possessing them is the ecstasy of detachment.

'Abdu'l-Bahá was not encumbered by His possessions. Well-to-do believers who visited the Master often brought gifts with them, which He graciously accepted. He would also generously pass on many such gifts to the poor. 'Abdu'l-Bahá appreciated beautiful things but did not feel obliged or compelled to hang on to them. We could learn from His example.

Commuting

I have a relative in London who commutes to work one and a half hours each way. That's three hours spent in his car and on a train every work day! He tells me that's not uncommon where he lives. I call it a formidable waste of time.

Suppose you commute one hour each direction. That is 500 hours a year in your car just to go to and from work. Isn't 500 hours worth asking yourself whether this is the only possible solution for you? Is there anything other than negotiating traffic that you would rather do with that time? Sleep, perhaps? Spend it with your loved ones? Unless you are a homefront pioneer, commuting is an enormous time-waster.

Mass commuting is a modern phenomenon. Living in place 'A' and driving to place 'B' every day while someone else lives in 'B' and drives to work in 'A' defies common sense. To be within a short walk, drive or bus ride to one's work, school and shops is better for the environment and for the soul.

In his book *Unless and Until(* subtitled *A Bahá'í Focus on the Environment)* Arthur Lyon Dahl describes right-sized communities which are likely to evolve as a new world order is established:

> In such a society, perfected systems of communications and transportation will render obsolete the need to crowd together in large cities. On the contrary, since energy and materials sources will be diffusely distributed across the

countryside, the human population could likewise be more widely spread. Community size will probably be determined by what the local resources can support and by what is the most agreeable size for social interactions. A community of a few thousand, for instance, would be large enough to provide basic social services such as education satisfactorily and economically, while permitting everyone to know everyone else, and thus be integrated fully into the life of the community.[4]

Doesn't *that* sound like the kind of community you want to live in? I believe we do not have to wait for the new world order to arrive before we start to experience some benefits of living in right-sized communities. Striving to live near our employment (or find employment closer to home) and giving our business to people in our own neighbourhoods are choices we can make right now.

Whenever I move I make an effort to get to know the service people, businesses and restaurants in my new neighbourhood. Though it can feel risky to start over with a new hairdresser or dentist, I feel good about supporting local businesses and I have met some wonderful people this way. People who strive to keep their business dealings within their own neighbourhoods are able to experience small-town cosiness within the big city.

One day while visiting Los Angeles I was stuck in traffic on a freeway. Eight lanes, not one of them moving. I looked up and saw a billboard above a new condominium complex under construction. It read: 'If you lived here, you'd be home by now!'

Television

> I must say I find television very educational.
> The minute somebody turns it on,
> I go to the library and read a good book.
> *Groucho Marx*

TV – Good Or Bad?

The number of hours people spend watching TV is indisputably rising. When I was a child we had a black and white television with two channels. We were constantly adjusting the antenna and the picture often rolled up or down. Nowadays there are cable and satellite systems that give viewers hundreds of choices of channels. Some of those choices are simplistic pollutants of the mind but some programming I must admit is quite outstanding.

A growing number of people believe that the television is an evil little box that pre-empts people from interacting with one another. It makes for socially stifled adults and children who lose their ability to initiate their own imaginative play. Instead, they sit and stare at a television screen. TV watchers are less interested in books and children's reading skills are not as well-developed as they could be. I know a few families who do not own televisions. I know many more who are striving to raise their children not to be TV dependent and strictly limit the number of hours they can watch. With groups like the TV-Turnoff Network springing up, it is becoming un-chic in some circles to admit you watch TV.

On the other hand, the quality of TV programming has advanced along with the quantity. While there is a lot of rubbish to sift through on the screen, there are now some remarkable educational programmes available. You can learn all about the cosmos, health, other cultures – the same quality of information offered by many educational institutions. This is the information age. If television is one of your sources for keeping up with information, I don't think you should be shy to admit it.

Even a little recreational TV is acceptable. Being a big *Law and Order* fan myself, I see the merits in television for occasional entertainment. If it's socially acceptable to go out to a movie, it should also be fine to watch a quality drama on TV once in a while. Only be concerned if you're spending more time with your fictional friends than you are with your real ones. I remain of the persuasion that a little TV watching is fine, if you choose your programmes wisely.

A meaner vice than television nowadays is the Internet, if you're spending too much time on it. We have a new social class of people – Internet widows and orphans – because someone in the family would rather be alone in his room with a computer than spend time with the family. And if you live alone, don't mistake web time for real human interaction. A lot of lonely and socially backward people prefer to communicate with others via the Internet. These people need friends and a good therapist.

While I praise television for the quality of much of the educational programming, one has to exercise more caution when using the Internet as a source of information. With the World Wide Web being so new and unregulated, there seems to be as much trash as there is reliable material. Anybody can put something on the

Internet: true, false or defamatory. Not everyone can successfully create and air a television programme though.

> Television has proved that people will look at anything
> rather than at each other.
> *Ann Landers*

TV Addiction

How can you tell if you are addicted to TV? You are an addict if:

- you leave your friends and rush home because your programme is on
- you leave the TV on and watch it with one eye when you have guests
- you're upset if your soap opera is pre-empted one day
- you discuss TV characters with friends as if they were real
- you are uncomfortable to be home alone, in silence

Television addiction is insidious. At first you think just watching a few minutes of a new show is harmless. Half an hour accidentally passes and you've watched the whole thing. If you watch the same show for 'a few minutes' again next week you get to know the characters better. Soon you are following the new show and have added that programme to your routine. The number of hours you watch every week increases and increases. There are some good programmes out there! One could watch all day.

My weakness is educational TV. I justify watching because I'm learning things. Great rationalization, huh? But do I really want to be a full-time television student on top of all the other roles I play in life? No! I give myself a weekly quota for TV time. If I get interested in a new weekly show, I have to drop another one off the menu.

Use your VCR as a time management tool. Programme it to tape your favourite shows and watch them later at times more convenient to you. Without watching the adverts, you save yourself even more time.

I complimented a Bahá'í friend of mine for not owning a television. I admired her for not pledging allegiance to the little box, as so many people have done. 'Oh, but I love watching TV!' she retorted. 'That's why I don't own one. I'd be watching it all the time!'

Motherhood

> . . . It is incumbent upon you to train the children from their earliest babyhood! . . . It is incumbent upon you to attend to them under all aspects and circumstances, inasmuch as God – glorified and exalted is He! – hath ordained mothers to be the primary trainers of children and infants. This is a great and important affair and a high and exalted position, and it is not allowable to slacken therein at all![5]

I suggest we do away with the term 'working mom'. Whether or not a woman has a job outside the home, does anyone know of a mother who *isn't* working? Michelle's story:

When my husband came home from work one day I asked him the usual 'How was your day?' We are both lawyers at the same firm. He told me about a new case the firm had taken on and the great luncheon meeting he had had with one of the partners. He then asked me what I had done that day. I really had to think, 'What *did* I do today?'

'I mailed a letter!' I said.

He stared patiently at me, waiting for the rest. There was no 'rest'. His eyebrows crept upward but he knew better than to say, 'You were home all day and only mailed a letter?' We both looked at our 12-month-old daughter, who was sitting innocently in her chair.

'I also scraped cereal off the high chair legs and washed it off the wall and out of my hair,' I added. 'I crawled around on the carpet and made animal noises. I put away the same toys 20 times though you'd never know it.' The house was in as much disarray as when he had left in the morning.

'So you were busy nurturing a member of the next generation of Bahá'u'lláh's servants,' he said. 'I'd say you made a bigger contribution to the world today than I did.'

I needed to hear that right then! I'm a first-time mother and sometimes miss the glamour of my other job. My current work clothes are T-shirts with spit-up on them. We had agreed that I would stay home as long as our finances would permit and then I'd prefer to go back to work part-time. We live in a society that admires mothers who stay home with their young children but society in general doesn't prioritize this function. Fortunately, as a Bahá'í mother I feel supported in my efforts to stay home with our daughter because the Bahá'í community reveres child-raising.

If Bahá'í parents do their job well, the result will be a better world for everyone. Remember to thank and support the parents you know for the sacrificial contributions they are making for us all. And give them a break by babysitting once in a while too!

Teaching Your Kids Time and Life Management Skills

Affluenza and hurry-sickness are new diseases of our generation. If you are feeling over-stressed and disorganized, what example are you setting for your children? You already know the unhappiness that chaos can bring into your own life and I trust you do not want your children to inherit your stress load. There are three important things you can do to prevent your children from becoming stressed-out, hurried adults.

First, look at the behaviours your children observe in you. If they often hear you say, 'I don't have time!' or 'I'm too busy!' or see you panic as you try to get ready to go out on time, they may take this information as what constitutes normal adult life. Then they will model it. Let your children observe in you someone who takes time for herself, someone who does not habitually take on too much and always feels behind, someone who is not so visibly stressed and always hurrying. Your serene example of living a walk-don't-run kind of life is one of the best gifts you can give your children. You would like your children to have balanced, healthy lives, wouldn't you? The fruits of your efforts will be evident in your children and grandchildren.

The results of the following study might surprise you. School-aged children with working parents were asked what their primary complaint was about their parents. It was *not* that their parents weren't home enough, although this was also true. The children's chief complaint was that their parents *brought their stress home.* The primary wish of today's children is not that their parents spend more time with them; they want their parents to please be less stressed when they *are* at home. Do we need to put that in bold for you?

Second, check if you are training your children to be over-loaded. Many well-intentioned parents have elected to enrol their children in several after-school programmes: sports, music, Scouts, language classes, drama, Bahá'í junior youth activities and so on. Parents say they have two primary motives. One is that they would simply like their children to have all the skills these organized activities offer. The second is that children who are busy with good things have less opportunity to flirt with temptation and be enticed by alcohol, drugs or crime. While both intentions are honourable, the parents need to be acutely conscious of not over-burdening their children. Too many activities for a young soul is detrimental to it. Do you want to teach your children to take on too much and become exactly like you? It is difficult to undo such a pattern when it is learned so young.

Child psychiatrists are now seeing adult-type stress disorders in children. This is a new problem, exclusive to the children of the hurry-sickness society. Too many organized activities and responsibilities are leading to anxieties in young people. Since children are not able to articulate 'I feel stressed', it comes out in the form of bed-wetting, stomach upset, nightmares, tantrums, withdrawal, to name a few symptoms. These overly-organized children lack time for unstructured play. A chance to just be kids. They are being turned into 'human doings' rather than allowed simply to be.

Third, give your children practical time and life management training from an early age. Some very prudent advice from a parenting expert: 'Once you teach your child to do something for himself, don't do it for him anymore.' Observe the animal kingdom. Once a mother animal has taught her young to hunt, she no longer does it for them. They need to practise their own survival skills. Once your child has learned how to pour his own cereal, that's his job now. The same is true for making his bed, packing his school lunch or doing his own laundry. Consider this: Your goal as a parent is to make your own job obsolete. Once you have raised a child to adulthood who can adequately care for himself you have succeeded as a parent. Having a 30-year-old son living at home where his cooking and laundry are done for him is not responsible parenting.

Hope

> Set all thy hope in God,
> and cleave tenaciously to His unfailing mercy.
> *Bahá'u'lláh*[6]

Where would we be without hope? Hopeless, I suppose, and that is a condition not worth living in. Without hope one is joyless and in darkness. The Oxford dictionary defines hope as 'a feeling of expectation and desire combined'. I feel happier just reading that. Hope suggests that a favourable resolve is around the corner, that good does prevail. Hope says that happiness is possible despite the drudgery that life sometimes brings.

Life is not one constant party. It is frequently painful

and regularly depressing. People who have a hopeful out-
look, however, are shielded from feeling many of life's
arrows. They recover from setbacks sooner. They see the
potential good in discouraging situations. They strive to
make themselves and others happy despite misfortune.

I believe that hope and optimism are choices we
make. We can elect to see the potential blessings in any
situation. Whether a person is facing a diagnosis of
cancer, struggling against poverty or facing an emotional crisis, there is always cause for hope. For when all
you have left is a hope and a prayer, you realize what
power there is in hope and prayer.

God grant me the strength to accept the things I cannot
change,
The courage to change the things I can,
And the wisdom to know the difference.
The Serenity Prayer

The Grunt Work

Do you ever get fed up with performing the tedious
tasks at home or at work? They are the not-so-glam-
orous jobs we all face at times. They are the tasks which
are often painstakingly slow, not to mention physically
or mentally strenuous. Here is a measuring stick to help
you determine if you are living within your purpose,
living in harmony with your 'To Be's:

When you are living with purpose,
you have an affection
for the grunt work involved.

Hence the writer who spends half a day researching in

a library and still does not find the item he wants, the dressmaker who chooses to crochet her own lace by hand, the archaeologist who spends years brushing dirt away from *possible* artifacts. All of these people face very tedious moments doing what they love but they are encouraged to continue because they see the connection between the grunt work and living the life they love.

> I would rather be a failure in something that I love
> than a success in something that I don't.
> *George Burns*

If you are cursing your tedious tasks, ask yourself, 'What is their greater purpose?' If there isn't one, or if the greater purpose doesn't resonate with who you want to be, then it may be time to make some changes. Hopefully, though, you can reconnect the link between your grunt work and your purpose, thereby having a new appreciation for it. No one really enjoys washing baby food off the kitchen floor four times in one day but being at home and watching your child grow is truly priceless.

Procrastination

Undone Tasks

Do you have a recurring item on your 'To Do' lists that you repeatedly avoid? Are you putting off cleaning the garage, for example, because you're overwhelmed by the size of the task? Break it down into small do-able portions. The first step might be just standing in the garage with a note pad, taking inventory of the steps involved. (Bottles can go to the recycling depot; old bike can be given to charity; skis can go up in the garage attic.) Fifteen minutes of inventory is all you do.

Next time, ask yourself, 'What will it take for me to move "garage cleaning" ahead one step?' and do one of the chores you listed. A few minutes of effort makes a visible difference where most projects are concerned, especially cleaning jobs. Taking a few steps, no matter how small, towards doing a task that has been looming over you starts to take the weight of the world off your shoulders.

If a 'to do' item remains continually untouched, there could be a good reason for it. Perhaps it doesn't have to be done. If you purchased fabric and a pattern several months ago (or even more than a year ago!), it is time to admit that sewing your own garment is not a priority for you. It is a nice dream, but 'seamstress' apparently doesn't rank very high on the list of who you want to be. Give the fabric to someone who will use it or pay a seamstress to sew your garment for you.

Re-evaluate all of your lingering undone tasks. Give yourself permission to let many of them go. Amazingly, the world will not end.

Right-Timing

Not all procrastination is bad. If you postpone writing a speech and then learn that the conference is cancelled anyway, you are saved from several hours of needless preparation. The difference between lazy procrastination and simply waiting is timing. You need to gauge when is the appropriate time to do something, then mark it on your calendar to be done. When you are procrastinating you know it by the twinge of guilt in your gut. Right-timing has no guilt; you are planning to start the item at the most reasonable time.

The frustration of doing something only to find out later it wasn't necessary escalates with the amount of valuable time that was sacrificed to do the task. This almost never occurs, however, when the tasks done contribute to who you want to be. If you want to be physically fit and you train for a ten kilometre race that gets rained out, you get to keep the well-conditioned body. The time spent training wasn't wasted. If 'I want to be a deepened Bahá'í' is on your 'To Be' list, then doing research for a deepening or fireside that gets cancelled is not a waste of time for you. You enjoyed doing the reading whether or not you used it in a talk.

Leaving It to the Last Minute

Leaving a task to the last minute isn't always procrastination. Some people perform very well when meeting deadlines. The adrenaline of racing against the clock brings out their creativity and they do their best work under these conditions. To test whether doing something just before it is due is your 'right-timing' or whether you are merely procrastinating, ask yourself the following:

Are you short-tempered or demanding with your co-workers or family members during this time?

Does your late work create stress or more work for someone else?

Do you show signs of physical or mental stress because of this schedule?

Do you wish you had more time so you could do a better job?

If you answered 'No' to all four questions, then you are someone whose 'right-timing' is often at the last minute. Enjoy your eccentricity and a job well done!

16

Words of Wisdom

Contrary to what readers might think, the greater challenge faced by most writers is not the task of composing and gathering enough material to comprise a whole book but rather in deciding which materials to *leave out*. This was especially true for this book. During final editing, many paragraphs, even chapters, ended up in the editing basket.

Victims of my editorial pen included quotations from some of history's greatest thinkers and writers. Some of their contributions were my personal favourites, which made editing even harder. While these quotations could not find a place in the text itself, I didn't want to deprive you of their wisdom and sometimes humour. I leave you now with a compilation of the more inspirational ones.

Being Here Now

The lure of the distant and the difficult is deceptive.
The great opportunity is where you are.
John Burroughs

Do not look back in anger, or forward in fear,
but around in awareness.
James Thurber

I never think of the future. It comes soon enough.
Albert Einstein

Boredom

Boredom: the desire for desires.
Leo Tolstoy

Courage

The only limit to our realization of tomorrow
will be our doubts of today.
Franklin Delano Roosevelt

Do not be too timid and squeamish about your action.
All life is an experiment.
Ralph Waldo Emerson

Creativity

Things don't turn up in this world until somebody turns
them up.
James Garfield

Genius means little more
than the faculty of perceiving in an unhabitual way.
William James

I am not a genius. I'm just a sponge.
I absorb ideas and put them in use.
Most of my ideas were thought of by somebody else,
who never bothered to develop them.
Thomas Edison

If I have ever made any valuable discoveries,
it has been owing to patient attention, than to any other
talent.
Sir Isaac Newton

If I have a thousand ideas a year and only one turns out to
be good,
I am satisfied.
Alfred Nobel

Men occasionally stumble over the truth,
but most of them pick themselves up and hurry off
as if nothing had happened.
Winston Churchill

Joy is but the sign that creative emotion is fulfilling its
purpose.
Charles Du Bois

Enthusiasm

Every production of genius must be the production of
enthusiasm.
Benjamin Disraeli

We act as though comfort and luxury were the chief
requirements of life,
when all that we need to make us happy is something to be
enthusiastic about.
Charles Kingsley

Excellence

If people knew how hard I had to work to gain my mastery,
it wouldn't seem wonderful at all.
Michelangelo

A specialist is someone who knows more and more about
less and less.
Dr William Mayo

Experience

Life is my college.
May I graduate well, and earn some honours.
Louisa May Alcott

Failure

If you have made mistakes, there is always another chance
for you.
You may have a fresh start any moment you choose,
for this thing we call failure is not the falling down, but the
staying down.
Mary Pickford

You cannot run away from a weakness;
you must sometime fight it out or perish;
and if that be so, why not now and where you stand?
Robert Louis Stevenson

Fear

Fear is nothing but faith in reverse gear.
The foundation on which both faith and fear rest is belief
in something.
Napoleon Hill

Fear is static that prevents me from hearing my intuition.
Hugh Prather

Fear is the main source of superstition,
and one of the main sources of cruelty.
To conquer fear is the beginning of wisdom.
Bertrand Russell

Focus

A man's education doesn't start until he finds what he
wants to learn.
Duke Ellington

I never could have done what I have done without the
habits
of punctuality, order and diligence,
without the determination to concentrate myself on one
subject at a time.
Charles Dickens

Concentrate all your thoughts upon the work at hand.
The sun's rays do not burn until brought to a focus.
Alexander Graham Bell

Follow Through

> To make your life a success, finish what you start.
> *Henry Ford*

> The great majority of men are bundles of beginnings.
> *Ralph Waldo Emerson*

Forgiveness

> To judge wisely, we must know how things appear to the unwise.
> *George Eliot*

Goals

> Give me a stock clerk with a goal
> and I will give you a man who will make history.
> Give me a man without a goal
> and I will give you a stock clerk.
> *J.C. Penney*

> Not having a goal is much more to be feared than not reaching a goal.
> *Robert Schuller*

> If you have built castles in the air, your work need not be lost;
> that is where they should be. Now put the foundations under them.
> *Henry David Thoreau*

The great thing in this world is not so much where we are,
but in what direction we are moving.
Oliver Wendell Holmes

Happiness

Happiness is a by-product, never a goal.
The person who sets out to seek happiness, never finds it.
Joyce Brothers

Most folks are as happy as they make up their minds to be.
Abraham Lincoln

Integrity

Integrity means a man is the same on the inside
as he claims to be on the outside.
Billy Graham

I like to see a man proud of the place in which he lives.
I like to see a man live so that his place will be proud of
him.
Abraham Lincoln

It is easier to fight for one's principles than to live up to
them.
Alfred Adler

Knowledge

As a general rule the most successful man
is the one who has the best information.
Benjamin Disraeli

Don't pretend to know more than you do.
Own up to your ignorance honestly,
and you will find people who are eager to fill your head
with information.
Walt Disney

Judge a man by his questions rather than by his answers.
Voltaire

Leadership

Leadership is the ability to decide what is to be done
and to get others to want to do it.
Dwight Eisenhower

Never tell people how to do things.
Tell them what to do and they will surprise you with their
ingenuity.
George Patton

Legacy

Our greatest responsibility is to be good ancestors.
Jonas Salk

Happiness is not enough. Honesty is not enough.
Man's aim must be the noble life devoted to the upraising
of humanity.
Vincent van Gogh

When you cease to make a contribution you begin to die.
Eleanor Roosevelt

Living the Life

I hope that if I'm ever arrested for being a Christian,
there'll be enough evidence to convict me.
Johnny Cash

I long to accomplish a great and noble task,
but it is my chief duty to accomplish small tasks
as if they were great and noble.
Helen Keller

It is easier to write ten volumes of philosophy
than to put one principle into practice.
Leo Tolstoy

To sensible men, every day is a day of reckoning.
John W. Gardner

Money

There are people who have money and people who are rich.
Coco Chanel

There is no dignity quite so impressive,
and no independence quite so important,
as living within your means.
Calvin Coolidge

Beware of little expenses; a small leak will sink a ship.
Ben Franklin

There is no reason to be the richest man in the cemetery.
You cannot do any business from there.
Harland Sanders

No one would have remembered the Good Samaritan
if he'd only had good intentions.
He had money as well.
Margaret Thatcher

The only wealth is life.
Henry David Thoreau

Obstacles

No one would ever have crossed the ocean
if he could have gotten off the ship in the storm.
Charles Kettering

Obstacles are those frightful things you see
when you take your eyes off your goal.
Henry Ford

Every adversity carries in itself
the seed of an equal or better advantage.
Napoleon Hill

To become a deeper man
is the privilege of those who have suffered.
Oscar Wilde

I know God will not give me anything I can't handle.
I just wish that He didn't trust me so much.
Mother Theresa

Optimism

A positive thinker does not refuse to recognize the negative;
he refuses to dwell on it.
Dr Norman Vincent Peale

Make the most of the best and the least of the worst.
Robert Louis Stevenson

I am an optimist. It does not seem too much use being anything else.
Sir Winston Churchill

Persistence

Effort only fully releases its reward after a person refuses to
quit.
Napoleon Hill

I never did anything worth doing by accident; they came by
work.
Thomas Edison

I start where the last man left off.
Thomas Edison

Prayer

Work as if you were to live 100 years.
Pray as if you were to die tomorrow.
Ben Franklin

Purpose

Life could be so wonderful if we only knew what to do
with it.
Greta Garbo

Every individual has a place to fill in the world,
and is important in some respect,
whether he chooses to be so or not.
Nathaniel Hawthorne

If a man love the labour of any trade
apart from any question of success or fame,
the gods have called him.
Robert Louis Stevenson

An aim in life is the only fortune worth finding;
and it is not to be found in foreign lands, but in the
heart itself.
Robert Louis Stevenson

If a man does not keep pace with his companions,
perhaps it's because he hears a different drummer.
Let him step to the music which he hears,
however measured or far away.
Henry David Thoreau

One can never consent to creep when one feels an
impulse to soar.
Helen Keller

All men should try to learn before they die
what they are running from, and to, and why.
James Thurber

Regret

Death is not the greatest loss in life.
The greatest loss is what dies inside us while we live.
Norman Cousins

Don't let yesterday use up too much of today.
Will Rogers

Religion

A man devoid of religion is like a horse without a bridle.
Abraham Lincoln

Role Models

Keep away from people who try to belittle your ambition.
Small people always do that,
but the really great make you feel that you, too, can
become great.
Mark Twain

Associate yourself with men of good quality if you esteem
your reputation;
for it's better to be alone than in bad company.
George Washington

Self Esteem

It is difficult to make a man miserable
while he feels he is worthy of himself
and claims kindred to the great God who made him.
Abraham Lincoln

Service

What do we live for,
if it is not to make life less difficult for each other?
George Eliot

Always do more than is required of you.
George Patton

I know of no great man
except those who have rendered great services
to the human race.
Voltaire

No person was ever honoured for what he received;
honour has been the reward for what he gave.
Calvin Coolidge

Silence

An inability to stay quiet
is one of the most conspicuous failings of mankind.
Walter Bagehot

Nowadays most men lead lives of noisy desperation.
James Thurber

The right words may be effective,
but no word was ever as effective as a rightly timed pause.
Mark Twain

Simplicity

Who is rich? He that rejoices in his portion.
Ben Franklin

Everything must be made as simple as possible
but not one bit simpler.
Albert Einstein

A man is rich in proportion to the number of things
which he can afford to let alone.
Henry David Thoreau

Solitude

The happiest of all lives is a busy solitude.
Voltaire

To do much clear thinking
a man must arrange regular periods of solitude
when he can concentrate and indulge his imagination
without distraction.
Thomas Edison

The best thinking has been done in solitude.
Thomas Edison

Success

Success seems to be connected with action.
Successful men keep moving.
They make mistakes, but they don't quit.
Conrad Hilton

The secret of success is constancy of purpose.
Benjamin Disraeli

Thinking

If everybody is thinking alike,
somebody isn't thinking.
George Patton

Thinking is the hardest work there is,
which is the probable reason why so few engage in it.
Henry Ford

The ancestor of every action is a thought.
Ralph Waldo Emerson

Time

Wasting time is much more sinful than wasting money.
Elizabeth Blackwell

We must use time as a tool, not as a couch.
John F. Kennedy

Truth

When you tell the truth you don't have to remember what
you said.
Mark Twain

This above all: to thine own self be true,
And it must follow, as the night the day,
That thou canst not then be false to any man.
William Shakespeare

Virtues

Just for today I will exercise my soul in three ways;
I will do somebody a good turn and not get found out;
I will do at least two things I don't want to do.
William James

Know yourself.
Don't accept your dog's admiration
as conclusive evidence that you are wonderful.
Ann Landers

You can experience success if you only focus
on possessing the virtues
that you would like your children to have.
Orison Swett Marden

Few men have virtues to withstand the highest bidder.
George Washington

What matters is not the idea a man holds,
but the depth at which he holds it.
Ezra Pound

The superior man thinks always of virtue;
the common man thinks of comfort.
Confucius

What Others Think

You wouldn't worry what other people thought of you
if you knew how seldom they did.
Anonymous

I don't know the key to success,
but the key to failure is trying to please everybody.
Bill Cosby

Women

Women are the greatest undeveloped natural resource
in the world today.
Edward Steichen

Work

Opportunity is missed by most people
because it is dressed in overalls and looks like work.
Thomas Edison

As we become drunkards by so many separate drinks,
so we become saints and authorities and experts
by so many separate acts and hours of work.
William James

If I have any success, it's due to luck,
but I notice the harder I work, the luckier I get.
Charles Kettering

A life not largely dedicated to vigorous, serious, useful work
cannot be happy and honourable.
Joseph Pulitzer

Work is not man's punishment.
It is his reward and his strength and his pleasure.
George Sand

Work keeps us from three great evils
– boredom, vice and need.
Voltaire

Don't go around saying the world owes you a living;
the world owes you nothing;
it was here first.
Mark Twain

Work is much more fun than fun.
Noel Coward

Worry

Nothing is worth worrying about.
I never worry, but I do become concerned.
Duke Ellington

All worry consumes, and to no purpose,
just so much physical and mental strength
that otherwise might be given to effective work.
Booker T. Washington

It all depends on how we look at things,
and not on how they are in themselves.
Carl Jung

If we could only rid ourselves of our imaginary troubles,
our lives would be infinitely happier and healthier.
Orison Swett Marden

17

The New You

In what ways are you different from when you first picked up this book? Do you have a clearer vision of the kind of person you aspire to be? Are the things you do each day in alignment with being that person? Have you adopted new techniques to keep your life simpler and better organized?

I hope so. Those were, I presume, your reasons for reading this book. If you have not yet changed your life as much as you had hoped, now is the best time to improve. Before this book gets put away on a shelf, go through it again and reread the parts you highlighted. Go through all the notes you made to yourself and see if there are any good ideas you liked but haven't implemented yet. If you don't start practising them now, there is even less of a chance that you will make the improvements later.

I am a different person for having written this book. I did not embark upon writing a time and life management book because I had my life so cleverly put together and thought I could rescue all the other busy Bahá'ís. I started researching life management strategies because I was a much too busy Bahá'í. I needed to bring my own life back to a saner pace. The more I researched and the more I practised new behaviours, the more I began to see the merits in there being a time and life management book tailored to Bahá'ís.

In the early weeks of turning over my new leaf, I had an exasperating moment looking for a lost piece of paper. It was a page buried in a pile of papers on my desk and was certainly taking more than the recommended 'less than 30 seconds' to find. I looked up from my mess and said to a visiting Bahá'í friend, 'What right do I have to write a book about time management? Look at me! I feel like a fat woman trying to write a diet book!'

She laughed at me. 'I think you should open your book with that line!' she said.

I considered her suggestion. Instead I'm closing with it. There's an expression 'We teach what we need to learn'. They say if you want to learn something really well, sign up to be an instructor for it. The preparation for the classes, the repetition of the lectures and the challenging questions presented by the students will teach you your subject extremely well. Personal time and life management was something I desperately wanted to learn.

If I was going to write and talk about having a well-organized home I would first need to have one myself. If I was going to recommend ways for Bahá'ís not to waste time each day on unimportant matters, I would first have to become faithful to the person I aspire to be. Doing the research for this book and changing my own lifestyle was the diet and exercise programme I needed to free myself from the chaos of my busy life. I am relieved to say that it *is* possible for a busy Bahá'í to regain control of her time and her life. If I can do it, I believe anybody who wants to also can.

Staying on Top

Depending on your degree of chaos, 'get organized' could be at the top of your 'To Do' lists for a while. It's fun to throw things out and buy new tools for organization! But getting organized does not mean disorder won't try to seep in again. Having an awesome filing system and the latest day-timer won't stop life from trying to get the better of you. Life is not static. It is constantly in a state of change and movement. Mail will continue to flow into your house, the telephone is going to ring, people will make urgent requests and dust will start to gather on your furniture the moment you've finished cleaning. It is not your goal to become totally stress-free. To be stress-free would mean being event-free and that is not possible.

It's okay to be busy. At least it is if you are enjoying yourself and are being responsible to your 'To Be's. Being excessively busy, however, particularly if you're doing the wrong things, is disloyal to oneself.

Time and life management training gives you the skills required to cope in a busy world. Applying small doses of *daily* maintenance is the way to keep on top of your life.

Staying Pumped

After attending a personal development seminar of any kind, people usually feel pumped. Hopefully the presenter was dynamic and the seminar was packed with useful advice. People walk out of the room feeling invigorated, vowing to practise everything they've just heard. Life is going to be noticeably different from now on! Research shows, however, the pumped feeling will start to fade the moment the participants leave the building. By the next day most of that enthusiasm could be gone. Only a few participants will actually put effort (and it does take effort) into re-reading their notes and practising what they have learned. These are the exceptional few who will go on to transform their lives.

Attending a personal development seminar or reading a book is akin to having a free trial workout with a personal trainer. After the workout session you are alive with the awareness of how good your life could be if you were to exercise every day.

Likewise, right now you are aware of how good your life could be if you were to stay organized. You are aware of what your life would look like if it were simplified and you stayed focused on your priority 'To Be's. Doing the following will help you stay pumped:

Leave this book and your personal notes out for a while where you will see them, as a reminder that improving your time and life management is a priority for you.

Every day take small steps to do things differently. If you habitually leave dishes in the living room after you snack, amaze yourself by putting them in the kitchen sink today.

Take small steps towards bigger projects. A fitness lifestyle change could begin today with ten sit-ups and five minutes of stretching.

Reflect on your 'Who I Aspire To Be' list every week. Imagining the best 'you' that you can possibly be will help you to stay focused and pumped.

Write daily 'To Do' lists, giving priority time to items that support your 'To Be's. Without guilt, let go of all the rest.

The person you aspire to be is a beautiful person! Look in the mirror right now and see all your potential looking back at you. You know what you need to do. Don't wait for tomorrow. Do something towards the new you TODAY!

The Beginning

Bibliography

'Abdu'l-Bahá. *Paris Talks*. London: Bahá'í Publishing Trust, 1967.
—— *Selections from the Writings of 'Abdu'l-Bahá*. Haifa: Bahá'í World Centre, 1978.

Bahá'í Prayers: A Selection of Prayers revealed by Bahá'u'lláh, the Báb and 'Abdu'l-Bahá. Wilmette, IL: Bahá'í Publishing Trust, 2002.

Bahá'í World Faith. Wilmette, IL: Bahá'í Publishing Trust, 2nd edn. 1976.

Bahá'u'lláh, *Gleanings from the Writings of Bahá'u'lláh*. Wilmette, IL: Bahá'í Publishing Trust, 1983.
—— *The Kitáb-i-Aqdas*. Haifa: Bahá'í World Centre, 1992.

Compilation of Compilations, The. Prepared by the Universal House of Justice 1963–1990. 2 vols. [Sydney]: Bahá'í Publications Australia, 1991.

Dahl, Arthur Lyon. *Unless and Until: A Bahá'í Focus on the Environment*. London: Bahá'í Publishing Trust, 1990.

Esslemont, J. E. *Bahá'u'lláh and the New Era*. London: Bahá'í Publishing Trust, 1974.

Lights of Guidance: A Bahá'í Reference File. Compiled by Helen Hornby. New Delhi: Bahá'í Publishing Trust, 5th edn. 1997.

Rabbaní, Rúḥíyyih. *The Priceless Pearl.* London: Bahá'í Publishing Trust, 1969.

References

1. Time Stress

1. 'Abdu'l-Bahá, *Selections*, p. 90.

2. To Be or Not To Be

1. Bahá'u'lláh, in *Bahá'í Prayers*, p. 4.
2. 'Abdu'l-Bahá, *Paris Talks*, p. 166.
3. Bahá'u'lláh, *Kitáb-i-Aqdas*, para. 33.

3. Much To Do About Everything

1. From a letter written on behalf of Shoghi Effendi to an individual, 6 March 1957, in *Lights of Guidance*, p. 248, no. 829.

5. Creating Balance

1. From a letter written on behalf of Shoghi Effendi to an individual, 25 October 1949, in *Lights of Guidance*, p. 280, no. 941. Emphasis added.

6. Organizing Your Home

1. From a talk of 'Abdu'l-Bahá, in *Lights of Guidance*, p. 220, no. 733.

9. Time Management for Your Health

1. 'Abdu'l-Bahá, in *Bahá'í Prayers*, p. 23.
2. 'Abdu'l-Bahá, *Paris Talks*, p. 175.

3. 'Abdu'l-Bahá, in Esslemont, *Bahá'u'lláh and the New Era*, p. 171.
4. 'Abdu'l-Bahá, in *Bahá'í World Faith*, p. 384.

10. Financial Management

1. Bahá'u'lláh, *Gleanings*, p. 276.
2. Bahá'u'lláh, *Kitáb-i-Aqdas*, para. 97.
3. Bahá'u'lláh, *Compilation*, vol. 1, pp. 497–8.
4. See a letter of Shoghi Effendi to the National Spiritual Assembly of Iran, 29 September 1942, in *Compilation*, vol. 1, p. 517.
5. From a letter of the Universal House of Justice to an individual, in *Lights of Guidance*, p. 306, no. 1036.
6. Bahá'u'lláh, *Kitáb-i-Aqdas*, para. 109.

11. Retirement

1. 'Abdu'l-Bahá, in *Compilation*, vol. 1, p. 313.
2. From a letter written on behalf of Shoghi Effendi, in *Kitáb-i-Aqdas*, note no. 56, p. 193.

12. Time Management for Bahá'í Administration

1. 'Abdu'l-Bahá, *Selections*, pp. 87–8.
2. From a letter of the Universal House of Justice to all National Spiritual Assemblies, 3 March 1977, in *Lights of Guidance*, p. 4, no. 14.

13. Administrative Efficiency

1. 'Abdu'l-Bahá, *Selections*, p. 87.
2. 'Abdu'l-Bahá, in *Compilation*, vol. 1, p. 96, no. 178.
3. From a letter written on behalf of Shoghi Effendi to an individual, 19 October 1947, in ibid. p. 106, no. 204.
4. 'Abdu'l-Bahá, *Selections*, p. 87.

14. Time Management for New Bahá'ís

1. From a letter written on behalf of Shoghi Effendi to an individual, 6 March 1949, in *Lights of Guidance*, pp. 343–4, no. 1150.
2. From a letter written on behalf of Shoghi Effendi to the National Spiritual Assembly of the United States, 10 January 1936, in *Lights of Guidance*, p. 234, no. 775.
3. From a letter of the Universal House of Justice to the National Spiritual Assembly of New Zealand, 28 December 1980, in ibid. p. 221, no. 734.
4. From a letter of the Universal House of Justice, 1 August 1978, in *Compilation*, vol. 1, p. 412, no. 914.

15. Short Subjects

1. Bahá'u'lláh, *Gleanings*, pp. 222–3.
2. 'Abdu'l-Bahá, in *Compilation*, p. 3, no. 13.
3. Rabbaní, *Priceless Pearl*, p. 201.
4. Dahl, *Unless and Until*, p. 55.
5. 'Abdu'l-Bahá, in *Lights of Guidance*, p. 149, no. 498.
6. Bahá'u'lláh, *Gleanings*, p. 323.